The Guardian

QUICK CROSSWORDS ^{BOOK} 4

Published in 2023 by Welbeck
An imprint of Welbeck Non-Fiction Limited
part of Welbeck Publishing Group
Offices in: London – 20 Mortimer Street, London W1T 3JW &
Sydney – Level 17, 207 Kent St, Sydney NSW 2000 Australia
www.welbeckpublishing.com

Puzzles © 2023 H Bauer Publishing
Design © 2023 Welbeck Non-Fiction,
part of Welbeck Publishing Group

Editorial: Millie Acers
Design: Bauer Media and Eliana Holder

A CIP catalogue for this book is available from the British
Library.

ISBN: 978-1-80279-428-1

Printed in the United Kingdom

10 9 8 7 6 5 4 3 2 1

The Guardian

QUICK CROSSWORDS BOOK 4

A collection of more than **200** engrossing puzzles

WELBECK

About the Guardian

The Guardian has published honest and fearless journalism, free from commercial or political interference, since it was founded in 1821.

It now also publishes a huge variety of puzzles every day, both online and in print, covering many different types of crosswords, sudoku, general knowledge quizzes and more.

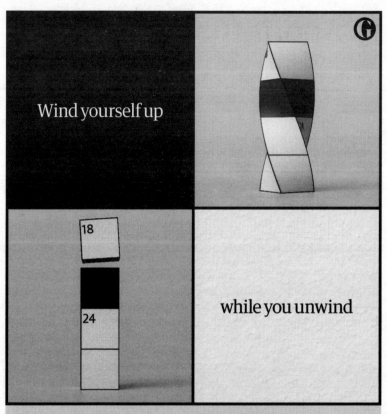

Introduction

Welcome to the fourth book in the *Guardian*'s challenging puzzle series. The humble quick crossword puzzle has appeared in the pages of the *Guardian* for decades, and these crosswords have been curated especially from recent issues to form a bumper batch of pure enjoyment.

These crosswords are designed to be solvable in a short time – there are not mountains of clues to work through. However, they are not easy. While a crossword expert may be able to solve them in a single break in the day, it is much more likely that you will have to step away and return to them later. Try it – your mind has a pleasantly surprising way of working on the answers without you even knowing.

Above all though, please enjoy this book! The world is full of challenges, but we hope that these challenges will provide a delightful diversion for you.

1

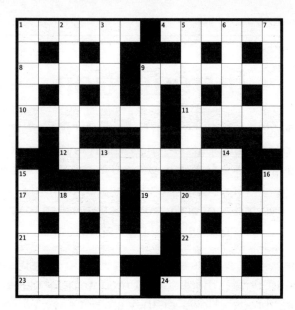

ACROSS

1 Medical condition caused by harmful bacteria in the blood (6)
4 Darker area (6)
8 Pale purple (5)
9 Diameter of a gun barrel (7)
10 ___ Lawson, cook (7)
11 American handbag — boxer's prize (5)
12 Flooded field for growing foodproducing swamp grass (4,5)
17 Eight musicians as a group (5)
19 Region of south-west France between the Bay of Biscay and the Pyrenees (7)
21 With no duty (3-4)
22 Like the moon (5)
23 Exhausted (6)
24 Host city for the 1896 Olympics (6)

DOWN

1 Signoret, de Beauvoir or Weil? (6)
2 One taking a dive (7)
3 Perfect in every way (5)
5 Adelphi (anag) — landing place (7)
6 Suspend (5)
7 Frankfurter (6)
9 Pale cream colour — map change(anag) (9)
13 Exclusive inner circle (7)
14 Cameroon's capital (7)
15 Spanish conquistador who toppled Montezuma, 1519 (6)
16 Mediterranean island country (6)
18 Poison (5)
20 Cut down the middle (5)

Solution see page 233

2

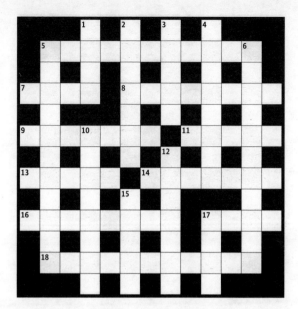

ACROSS

- **5** A soft-centred chocolate (6,5)
- **7** Shame (4)
- **8** Selfish drivers (4,4)
- **9** Tenpin (7)
- **11** Loose dress for a woman or child (5)
- **13** Trap (5)
- **14** Showing great enthusiasm (7)
- **16** Very hot curry (8)
- **17** Traditional kind of music (4)
- **18** The same length away (11)

DOWN

- **1** Shop selling alcohol for drinking elsewhere (informal) (4)
- **2** In a very odd way (7)
- **3** Do away with (5)
- **4** Traditional kind of white sauce — calm Hebe (anag) (8)
- **5** Galvanised network with a hexagonal mesh (7,4)
- **6** Remedy that prevents or solves a problem (5,6)
- **10** Shattered (5,3)
- **12** Great bravery (7)
- **15** Glasgow's river (5)
- **17** Textile fibre (4)

Solution see page 233

3

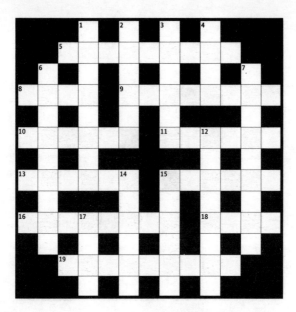

ACROSS

5 Gluttonous (9)

8 Good heavens! (4)

9 Long programme broadcast to raise money for a cause (8)

10 Nasty and unpleasant (6)

11 Protruding belly (6)

13 Move fast (and naked?) (6)

15 Delight (6)

16 In the adjoining house (4,4)

18 In bad taste (4)

19 Scrumptious (9)

DOWN

1 Conviviality (8)

2 Food storeroom (6)

3 Boost (6)

4 Broken (informal) (4)

6 Ostracised (9)

7 Grant condescendingly — have focus (anag) (9)

12 Computer ID (8)

14 Tricky (to untangle?) (6)

15 Word group (6)

17 Removed (4)

Solution see page 233

4

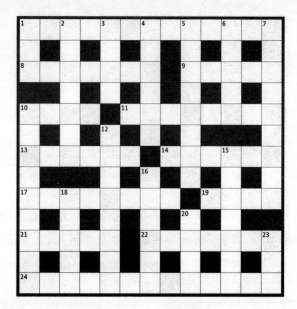

ACROSS

1 Resonance (13)
8 Long and hollow (7)
9 Punctuation mark (5)
10 Wharf (4)
11 Joyous emotion (8)
13 Causing wry amusement (6)
14 US space programme, 1961–72 (6)
17 Circular piece of hair pressed against forehead (4,4)
19 Discharge (4)
21 Oklahoma city — salut (anag) (5)
22 Fabric with raised pattern — co-ed bar (anag) (7)
24 Prank (9,4)

DOWN

1 Putrefaction (3)
2 Pulsating musical effect (7)
3 Have confidence (in) (4)
4 Bawdy (6)
5 Sweet spirit-based drinks marketed for the young (8)
6 Dwelling in the far north (5)
7 Kid's mother? (5,4)
10 Lively ballroom dance (9)
12 Graph with circle divided into proportional sectors (3,5)
15 Lower back pain (7)
16 Middle East and North African language (6)
18 Saucy dance? (5)
20 Vote (4)
23 Sheep (3)

Solution see page 233

5

ACROSS

1 Commandeer illegally (6)
4 Substitute GP (5)
7 Swallow up (6)
8 Kind of bean (6)
9 Neé (4)
10 Carrying too much weight above (3–5)
12 Throwing spirit? (11)
17 Underhand behaviour (8)
19 Drop down (4)
20 Troublemaker (6)
21 On the same side (6)
22 Painter's stand (5)
23 Bony (6)

DOWN

1 Chicken house (3,4)
2 Diary (7)
3 Coffee pot with plunger (9)
4 Chuckle out loud (5)
5 Tout for custom (7)
6 Person dying for a cause (6)
11 Pot for saving pennies? (9)
13 Forbidding (7)
14 Sugar-regulating hormone (7)
15 Where animal hides are treated (7)
16 Lack enough food (6)
18 Toll (5)

Solution see page 234

6

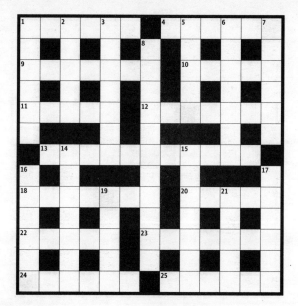

ACROSS

1 Hold tight (6)
4 River — plant (6)
9 Endless (7)
10 True (5)
11 Not justified (5)
12 Promote (7)
13 Miscellaneous collection (4,3,4)
18 Adventure (7)
20 Out of sight of land? (2,3)
22 Shell out (5)
23 Hamlet (7)
24 Mountain range (6)
25 Swedish coins (6)

DOWN

1 Little angel (6)
2 Overturn (5)
3 Come clean (7)
5 City on Eurostar routes from London to Paris and Brussels (5)
6 Perverse (7)
7 Stand-in (6)
8 Unconventional — tea interval (anag) (11)
14 Run down (7)
15 One makes things possible (7)
16 Against (6)
17 Hurtle (6)
19 Getting on (5)
21 Fish eggs (5)

Solution see page 234

7

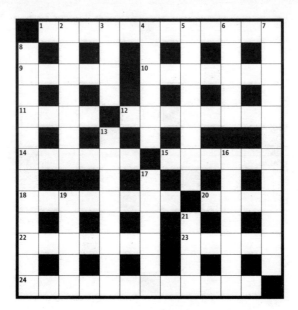

ACROSS

1 Critical (3–9)
9 Original — book (5)
10 Establish (7)
11 Gown (4)
12 Approving gesture (6–2)
14 Wobble (6)
15 Spanish dictator, d. 1975 (6)
18 Military commander's aide (8)
20 Prune (4)
22 Anger (7)
23 Female relative (5)
24 Impenetrable jargon (12)

DOWN

2 Endearing (7)
3 Futile — lazy (4)
4 Predicament (6)
5 Evergreen herb (that's for remembrance) (8)
6 Gather (5)
7 Autocue (12)
8 Obsequious (12)
13 Lookout (8)
16 Having a positive or negative value (3–4)
17 Plan (6)
19 Esau's brother, who dreamed of a way to climb to heaven (5)
21 Warm and comfortable (4)

Solution see page 234

8

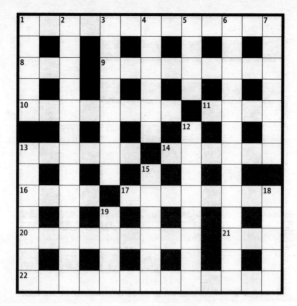

ACROSS

1 They direct drivers — right at cliffs (anag) (7,6)
8 Fast-running, flightless bird (3)
9 Celebratory drink (9)
10 Valuable (8)
11 Substitute (4)
13 Song by The Doors (1967) and The Beatles (1969) (3,3)
14 Died down (6)
16 Greek letter I (4)
17 Ruminated (8)
20 Popular drama (4,5)
21 Social insect (3)
22 Mock (4,3,6)

DOWN

1 Fool (5)
2 Fun place for thrill-seekers (9,4)
3 Splinter groups (8)
4 Stop talking (4,2)
5 Observational game for children (1-3)
6 Apex (4-5,4)
7 Saturated (7)
12 Capital of the United Arab Emirates (3,5)
13 Matching knitwear (7)
15 Sailor, b. 1929, who ate spinach (6)
18 Eccentric (5)
19 Foundation (4)

Solution see page 234

9

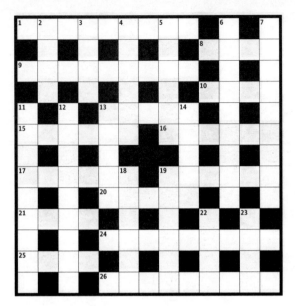

ACROSS

1 That's absurd! (4,3,2)
8 Intelligence (abbr) (4)
9 Determine (9)
10 Selfless knights of Star Wars (4)
13 Tribunal (5)
15 Recovery from a low point (6)
16 Classical composition with an instrumental soloist (6)
17 Trounce (6)
19 Cream-filled choux pastry (6)
20 Plant-derived dye for hair or skin (5)
21 Contribute to a common fund (4)
24 Form (9)
25 Tender (4)
26 Forestalled (9)

DOWN

2 All right (4)
3 Apiece (4)
4 Intense (4-2)
5 Buries (6)
6 Occurring before birth (9)
7 Diamond in a setting by itself (9)
11 Place side by side (9)
12 Right side of a ship (9)
13 Collapse (5)
14 Puccini opera of 1900 (5)
18 Device that warms (6)
19 Stand (6)
22 Where to board a bus (4)
23 Encourage (4)

Solution see page 235

10

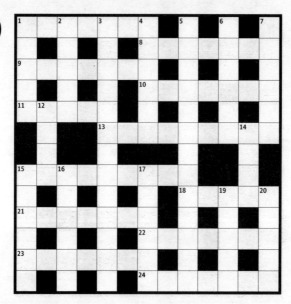

ACROSS

1 Post-1947 tension between the Soviet Union and the United States and their allies (4,3)

8 Not in anyone's possession (7)

9 Infection of the nervous system from germs in open wounds — eat nuts (anag) (7)

10 Capital of Georgia (7)

11 Relating to sound (5)

13 Swing back and forth (9)

15 Winner's trophy (4,5)

18 Irritating (5)

21 Munster (anag) — flat bone in the chest (7)

22 Clear (7)

23 Dilettante (7)

24 Bizarre (7)

DOWN

1 Makes a reference (to) (5)

2 Admit (3,2)

3 RAF equivalent to a British army lieutenant colonel (4,9)

4 Pastoral (6)

5 Person seeking to go up in the world (6,7)

6 Heart condition (6)

7 Recommendation (6)

12 Spiced stew of various meats and vegetables (4)

14 Piffle (4)

15 One cannot stop talking (informal) (6)

16 Room for manoeuvre (6)

17 Takes exception (6)

19 Duplicate (5)

20 Bumpkin (5)

Solution see page 235

11

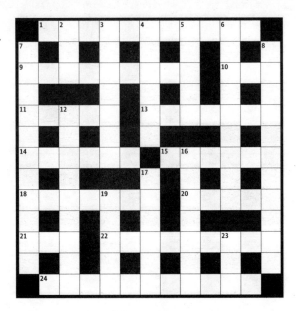

ACROSS

1 Showing off — nine tattoos (anag) (11)

9 Breed (9)

10 Excessively (3)

11 Conifer (of Lebanon?) (5)

13 Kind (7)

14 Summarises briefly (abbr) (6)

15 Straight sword with a narrow two-edged blade (6)

18 Corpse (7)

20 Correct (5)

21 Flow (3)

22 Infamous (9)

24 Substitute (11)

DOWN

2 Placatory concession (3)

3 Narcissistic venture (3,4)

4 Platitude (6)

5 Subject (5)

6 In an unstable position (2,4,3)

7 Past performance (5,6)

8 Hot sauce, popular with beef-eaters (11)

12 Immorality (9)

16 A puzzling combination of letters? (7)

17 Professional judge (6)

19 Corrupt (5)

23 Personal (3)

Solution see page 235

12

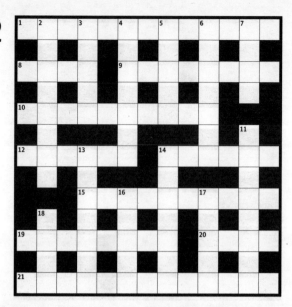

ACROSS

1 Alarm (13)
8 Writer (4)
9 Proclaimed (8)
10 Sidestep (10)
12 Stuff (6)
14 Neglect (6)
15 Naively optimistic (6–4)
19 Hard wheat flour used in pasta and puddings (8)
20 Great rage (4)
21 Senior barrister (6,7)

DOWN

2 Fresh and unusual (8)
3 Long–suffering (5)
4 Characteristic of a certain area (7)
5 Slot (5)
6 Farm vehicle (7)
7 Surplus (4)
11 Run through (8)
13 Put back (7)
14 Jumble (7)
16 Wrong (5)
17 Small and delicate (5)
18 List of options (4)

Solution see page 235

13

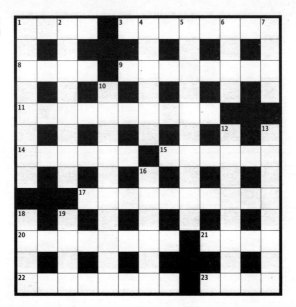

ACROSS

1 Skin (4)
3 Inappropriate (8)
8 Large bag made of hessian, for example (4)
9 Sealed (8)
11 Documents proving who did what (5,5)
14 Trim (6)
15 American actor, awarded Oscar for Best Actor in Scent of a Woman in 1993 (6)
17 Patchy (3-3-4)
20 Journey's end (or beginning) (8)
21 Finance (4)
22 Honeymooner (5-3)
23 Take notice (4)

DOWN

1 Travel document (8)
2 Lark — spade ace (anag) (8)
4 Catchphrase (6)
5 Ticks off (10)
6 Feel yearning (4)
7 Lacking refinement (4)
10 Inclination (10)
12 Make fun of (8)
13 Unbalanced (8)
16 Greeting (6)
18 Shock (4)
19 Pull (a revolver?) (4)

Solution see page 236

14

ACROSS

1 Dissolute (10)

7 Wholesome — well-groomed (5-3)

8 Run briskly (4)

9 Catch on belatedly (informal) (4)

10 Significant (7)

12 Pragmatic guideline (4,2,5)

14 Fun activity (7)

16 Rewrite (4)

19 Carbonated drink (4)

20 Punters may pay for their advice (8)

21 Poisonous New World spider (5,5)

DOWN

1 Glazed white and blue earthenware (5)

2 Lacking any warmth or friendliness (7)

3 Small cut (4)

4 Goes back (8)

5 Completely wreck — the lot (5)

6 Socialise (with) (6)

11 Superficial (8)

12 Argue (6)

13 Modernised (7)

15 Follow — path (5)

17 Light cloth covering for furniture (5)

18 Vomit (4)

Solution see page 236

15

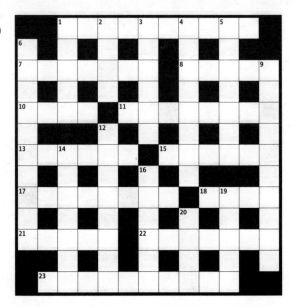

ACROSS

1 Keep going (10)
7 Pariah (7)
8 Promotional words on a book jacket (5)
10 Plug used to stop a hole (4)
11 Nit-picking (8)
13 Leading authority (6)
15 Cheapen (6)
17 National flower of Wales (8)
18 Hit hard (4)
21 Practice session (5)
22 Spend extravagantly (7)
23 Writing materials (10)

DOWN

1 Hoax (3-2)
2 Genuine (4)
3 Each of two (6)
4 Not defeated (8)
5 Legal custodian (7)
6 Passionate (3-7)
9 Old newspaper or periodical (4,6)
12 Illuminated at night (8)
14 Trouble (7)
16 Shambles (6)
19 Make haste (5)
20 Inkling (4)

Solution see page 236

16

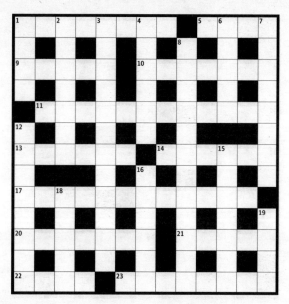

ACROSS

1 Theatrical (8)
5 Make the grade (4)
9 Fastener (5)
10 Vessel used for deepening a channel (7)
11 Atmosphere (12)
13 Clear and bright (6)
14 Covered way with shops (6)
17 Painter's tool (7,5)
20 Yet (7)
21 Soak thoroughly (5)
22 Scandal (4)
23 Small bit (8)

DOWN

1 It's on the menu (4)
2 Laser or Nato, for instance (7)
3 Full of gratitude (12)
4 Cause (6)
6 Fish with a hook (5)
7 White wine and soda water (8)
8 Tragic — Ann hid regret (anag) (12)
12 Careless (8)
15 Good-humoured (7)
16 Badly-behaved child (6)
18 Depress (5)
19 Depression (4)

Solution see page 236

17

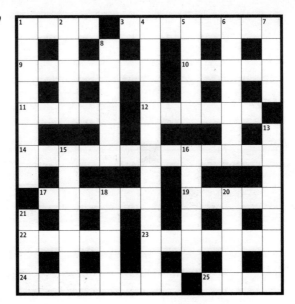

ACROSS

1 Shipshape (4)
3 Branch (8)
9 Ceremonial finery (7)
10 Live in someone else's home (5)
11 Stretched (5)
12 Out of sight (6)
14 Having influential friends (4-9)
17 Start up (6)
19 Lucky accident (5)
22 Begin again (5)
23 La Bohème composer (7)
24 Troublesome (8)
25 Previously (4)

DOWN

1 Decline (4,4)
2 Fixed belief (5)
4 Short-lived success (5,2,3,3)
5 Like a rock (5)
6 Unused piece (7)
7 Long journey (4)
8 Health centre (6)
13 Sticky substance (8)
15 Novice (7)
16 Totally rub out (6)
18 I don't believe it! (2,3)
20 Workers' organisation (5)
21 Make tea (or something stronger?) (4)

Solution see page 237

18

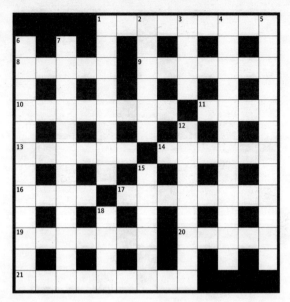

ACROSS

1 Decipher (6,3)
8 Part of a long poem (5)
9 Child's first outfit? (7)
10 Opinions (8)
11 Slight (4)
13 Make public (6)
14 Ruffle (6)
16 Top edge of a container (4)
17 Murderous feud (8)
19 Galvanise (7)
20 Conjure up (5)
21 Slack (9)

DOWN

1 Thrive (8)
2 Drinking vessel (6)
3 Bones protecting the heart and lungs (4)
4 Arrangement (12)
5 Agent provocateur (12)
6 Absent-minded person (12)
7 Resourceful (12)
12 Practical trial under realistic working conditions (4,4)
15 Obliterate (6)
18 Pen-name of short story writer HH Munro, d. 1916 (4)

Solution see page 237

19

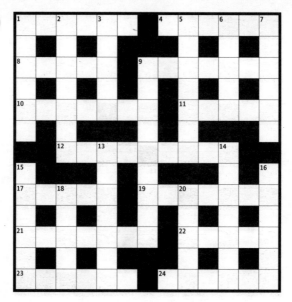

ACROSS

1 Dupe (6)
4 Mind (6)
8 Sinister (5)
9 Green fields (7)
10 One pops up for breakfast (7)
11 Superior — drug (5)
12 Deadlock (9)
17 Subsequently (5)
19 Very unusual (7)
21 Extract from a text (7)
22 Belong (3,2)
23 Favour (6)
24 Structure designed to slow coastal erosion (6)

DOWN

1 Afternoon nap (6)
2 Body (7)
3 Elite (5)
5 Utensil with a wide flat blade (7)
6 Munch (5)
7 Make certain (6)
9 Communication system — cede rooms (anag) (5,4)
13 Cost of flying (7)
14 That's just it! (7)
15 Excellent and lavish (informal) (4-2)
16 Quick look (6)
18 Experience — discrimination (5)
20 Put off (5)

Solution see page 237

20

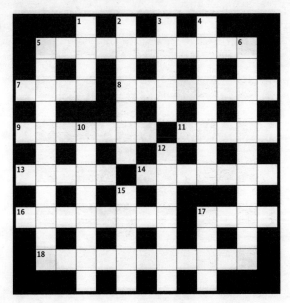

ACROSS

5 Toady (5,6)
7 Throng (4)
8 Rosa isn't (anag) — criminal (8)
9 Forceful and rigorous (7)
11 It may be twirled (or passed!) (5)
13 Resources (5)
14 Unsophisticated (7)
16 Extra something (8)
17 What's owing (4)
18 Main body of any group (4,3,4)

DOWN

1 Conflict (4)
2 Go-getting (7)
3 Stern (5)
4 Local government headquarters (4,4)
5 Vocal supporter (11)
6 Conscientious — to blame (11)
10 Conscious (8)
12 Explosive device (7)
15 Last round (5)
17 Feeble character (4)

Solution see page 237

21

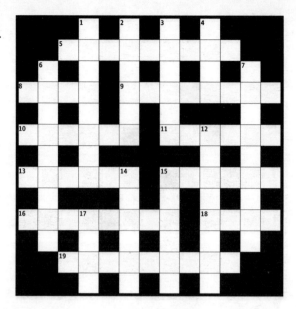

ACROSS

5 Minder (9)
8 Open wide (4)
9 Hope for the future (8)
10 Moves (6)
11 Spring back (6)
13 Deft (6)
15 Wait a minute! (4,2)
16 To the point (8)
18 Self-satisfied (4)
19 Extremely violent (9)

DOWN

1 Backwards and forwards (2,3,3)
2 Avoid — surgical procedure (6)
3 Saddle (6)
4 Document issued by a court (4)
6 Faded (by sunlight) (6,3)
7 Actor's revealing monologue (9)
12 The one at Rhodes was one of the Seven Wonders of the World (8)
14 Inferior (6)
15 Empty words (3,3)
17 Bite (the cud?) (4)

Solution see page 238

22

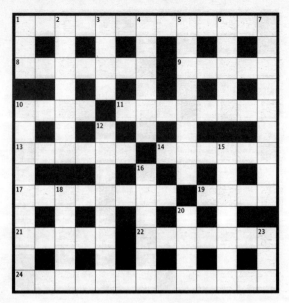

ACROSS

1 Classroom stand-in (6,7)

8 Piece of ground with specific characteristics (7)

9 Criminal twins, Ronnie and Reggie (5)

10 Goddess of the rainbow and messenger of the Titans (4)

11 Contaminated (8)

13 Astringent substance in tea and wine (6)

14 Colours flown at sea to indicate nationality (6)

17 Determined (8)

19 Mediterranean meal of many small dishes (4)

21 Hebridean island, known for its malt whisky distilleries (5)

22 Allowed (7)

24 Old way for constructing internal walls — tabulated wand (anag) (6,3,4)

DOWN

1 Command to a trained dog (3)

2 Helping of food (7)

3 Make available for a limited time (4)

4 Speaker system (6)

5 Not acidic (8)

6 Core (5)

7 Home (9)

10 Quiz (9)

12 Treacherous (8)

15 Lack of initiative (7)

16 Shame (6)

18 Sound of something soft and wet hitting a surface (5)

20 Unvarnished (4)

23 Wipe (3)

Solution see page 238

23

ACROSS

1 Arctic permafrost region (6)
4 Eagerly absorb (3,2)
7 Set-to (informal) (4-2)
8 Partisan (6)
9 Equitable (4)
10 Drive out (8)
12 Incompatible (3-8)
17 Struggle awkwardly (8)
19 Hilltop (4)
20 Seeds used to make tahini (6)
21 Strengthened opening for a lace (6)
22 Become widespread on social media (5)
23 Suppose (6)

DOWN

1 Sea wave caused by an earthquake (7)
2 Instinctive (7)
3 Inhibited (9)
4 Moon-related (5)
5 Nutty confectionery (7)
6 Hotel or hospital employee (6)
11 Old US rose (anag) — without scent (9)
13 Once-over (informal) (4-3)
14 Theatrical group of motionless figures (7)
15 Bishop's patch (7)
16 Balance (6)
18 Known as (5)

Solution see page 238

24

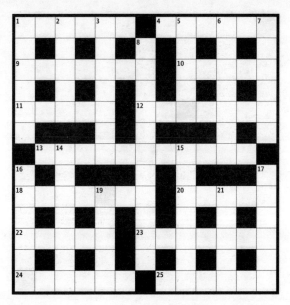

ACROSS

1 Area of muddy or boggy ground (6)
4 Deplorable (6)
9 The Treasure State (7)
10 Should (5)
11 Indian monetary unit (5)
12 Alumni (3,4)
13 Large bird found in mountainous parts of the northern hemisphere (6,5)
18 Climb with difficulty (7)
20 One who's up? (5)
22 Sticky substance exuded by fir trees (5)
23 Wide area (7)
24 Less burdensome (6)
25 A horse (anag) — on the beach? (6)

DOWN

1 ROM or RAM (6)
2 Preliminary period (3-2)
3 Marine algae (7)
5 Egg-shaped (5)
6 Type of biscuit (3,4)
7 Most recent (6)
8 Systematic attempt to undermine opponents' morale (3,2,6)
14 Aristotle __ , Greek shipping magnate, d.1975 (7)
15 To the point (7)
16 Accumulate (6)
17 English novelist, Graham, d. 1991 (6)
19 Head (slang) (5)
21 Haven't a clue! (informal) (5)

Solution see page 238

25

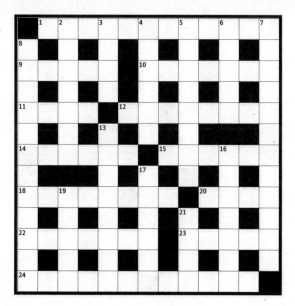

ACROSS

1 US November national holiday (12)

9 European money (5)

10 Storehouse for threshed wheat etc (7)

11 Hector's city (4)

12 Squadron of small warships (8)

14 Public school — clod breaker (6)

15 Made level (6)

18 Outside-wall covering (8)

20 Klemperer, Preminger or Bismarck? (4)

22 Venezuelan river (7)

23 Afghan capital (5)

24 Yield to authority (7,5)

DOWN

2 Secretly shelter (7)

3 Anglo-Welsh dandy, d. 1762 — American poet, d. 1971 (4)

4 In a wise way (6)

5 Dormant (8)

6 With everything considered (2,3)

7 1950 musical based on Damon Runyon short stories (4,3,5)

8 Succeed in a race against time (4,3,5)

13 Game bird (8)

16 Of significance (7)

17 Forty winks (6)

19 Parting word (5)

21 Analogous (4)

Solution see page 239

26

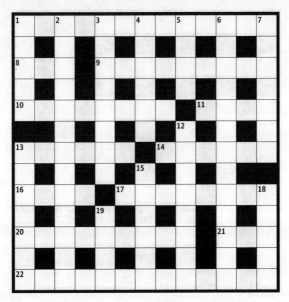

ACROSS

1 Fierce conflict (7,6)

8 Court (3)

9 Over a considerable distance (4-5)

10 Unauthorised passenger (8)

11 Thomas Hardy's 'obscure' protagonist (4)

13 Asian temple (6)

14 One taking pleasure from the suffering of others (6)

16 Light toboggan (4)

17 Pain — check a BA (anag) (8)

20 Small sausage — poach tail (anag) (9)

21 Devon's main river (3)

22 Not special or noteworthy (2,5,6)

DOWN

1 Welsh county (5)

2 Out-and-out (13)

3 French president, 2012-17 (8)

4 Shakespeare's fictional king of Scotland in Macbeth (6)

5 City site of the Taj Mahal (4)

6 Jokingly (6-2-5)

7 Mountain on the Nepal-Tibet border (7)

12 Repercussion (8)

13 Bird with a big bill (7)

15 Empty (6)

18 Numbers divisible by two (5)

19 Downward-facing concave shape (4)

Solution see page 239

27

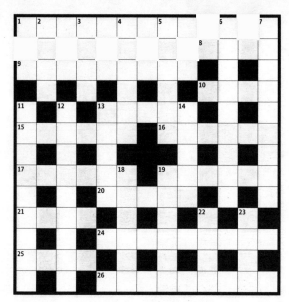

ACROSS

1 Drip's name (anag) — superhero (6-3)
8 Jab (4)
9 Blows to the chin (9)
10 Charitable donation(s) (4)
13 Make contact (5)
15 Brighton & Hove or West Bromwich FC (6)
16 Fully informed (French) (2,4)
17 Fur shoulder cape (6)
19 Real (6)
20 Soggy ground (5)
21 Well-behaved (4)
24 Tetchy (9)
25 Drew (4)
26 Spying (9)

DOWN

2 Tube for conveying gas or liquid (4)
3 Eating regime (4)
4 Figure out (6)
5 Athens' region — New York prison (6)
6 Workmate (9)
7 Adapting easily to different tasks (9)
11 Censure severely (9)
12 Analgesic and anti-inflammatory drug (9)
13 Object with ritual significance (5)
14 Idea based on intuition (5)
18 Sign of the zodiac (6)
19 Home of St Francis (6)
22 Minor chess piece (4)
23 Wooden-soled shoe (4)

Solution see page 239

28

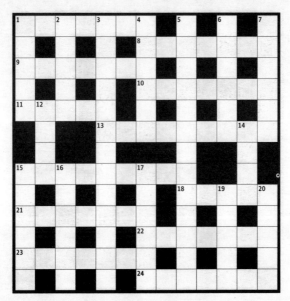

ACROSS

1 Twin-purpose furniture item (4,3)
8 Self-centredness (7)
9 Kind of paint (7)
10 Whistler and Piper, say (7)
11 Ancient Greeks' abode of the dead (5)
13 Random (9)
15 Fine-tune — bacterial (anag) (9)
18 Wealthy man (returning from India with a fortune?) (5)
21 Small dwelling (7)
22 Starting points (7)
23 Enjoying a winning streak (2,1,4)
24 Underground prison (7)

DOWN

1 Squirrel away (5)
2 Set alight (5)
3 Zebra crossing indicator (7,6)
4 Abscond (6)
5 Infringement (13)
6 Elaborate outdoor party (6)
7 Diverted (6)
12 Verdi opera (4)
14 Nevada divorce city (4)
15 Wrap up gently for protection (6)
16 Deadly (6)
17 Ancient (3-3)
19 Corrupt inducement (5)
20 Bathroom sink (5)

Solution see page 239

29

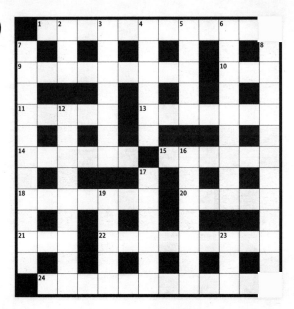

ACROSS

1 Royal Navy flag (5,6)
9 French emperor (9)
10 Pull along (3)
11 Something from the distant past (5)
13 Free from pressure — ease (7)
14 Robustly masculine (6)
15 Lust (6)
18 Pestered (7)
20 Morally defensible (5)
21 Break a fast (3)
22 Infancy (9)
24 Bonn was its capital (4,7)

DOWN

2 Feathered layer? (3)
3 Characteristic (7)
4 Boobs (6)
5 Pinch (5)
6 Assembly (9)
7 Shortened (11)
8 The Demon Barber of Fleet Street (7,4)
12 Pair of glasses with a handle (9)
16 Rank of a hereditary peer, husband of a countess (7)
17 Give guidance (6)
19 Sailing boat (5)
23 Possess (3)

Solution see page 240

30

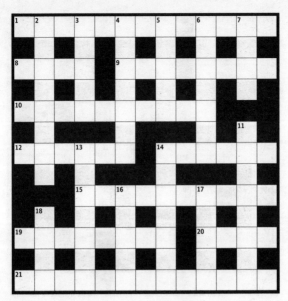

ACROSS

1 At last! (3,6,4)
8 Marijuana (slang) (4)
9 Cause for serious concern (8)
10 Overall sum (5,5)
12 Influenced (6)
14 Seek to persuade, repeatedly and annoyingly (6)
15 Aggravate (10)
19 Significant feature (or event) (8)
20 Gone (4)
21 Thoroughly (4,3,6)

DOWN

2 A few (3,2,3)
3 46th president of the United States (5)
4 Ate lavishly (7)
5 Sunday meal, perhaps (5)
6 Fell (7)
7 In pristine condition (4)
11 Period of unusually warm weather (4,4)
13 Gave way (7)
14 Separate (5,2)
16 For the second time (5)
17 Longest running British children's comic (5)
18 Salad dressing (abbr) (4)

Solution see page 240

31

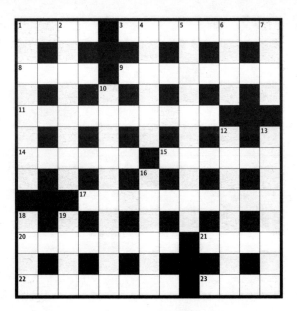

ACROSS

1 Blast of wind (4)
3 Fitted out (8)
8 Type of tide (4)
9 Pepper plant — mica cups (anag) (8)
11 Vulnerable spot (10)
14 Most insignificant (6)
15 Two-channel sound (6)
17 Branch of science concerned with earthquakes (10)
20 Canadian federal police (8)
21 Something never to be done (2-2)
22 Fair (8)
23 Refuse to acknowledge (4)

DOWN

1 Card game (3,5)
2 Norm(al) (8)
4 Member of the Religious Society of Friends (6)
5 Heat-loss prevention (10)
6 Dark red or purple-brown (4)
7 Moist (4)
10 Searcher for minerals (10)
12 Wood preservative (8)
13 Plump — podgy (4-4)
16 Express agreement (6)
18 Muslim community leader (4)
19 Felt remorse (for) (4)

Solution see page 240

32

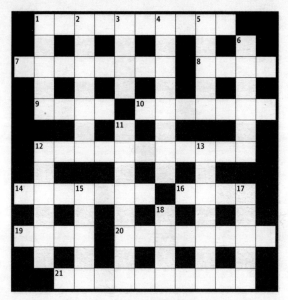

ACROSS

1 Obsequiousness (10)
7 Stanza of four lines (8)
8 Roam (4)
9 Small amount of liquid (4)
10 Easily broken (7)
12 Comfort after loss or disappointment (11)
14 Important person (3,4)
16 Snug retreat (4)
19 Traditional fuel from a bog (4)
20 Powerless (8)
21 Garfunkel song from the 1978 soundtrack of Watership Down (6,4)

DOWN

1 Group of soldiers — team of players (5)
2 Reduce (3,4)
3 French chanteuse (the Little Sparrow), d. 1963 (4)
4 Atypical (8)
5 Mark indicating text insertion (5)
6 Place to which the dead King Arthur was conveyed (6)
11 Driving a car (8)
12 Wound up — docile (anag) (6)
13 In a maladroit manner (7)
15 Lecherous man (5)
17 North African capital (5)
18 Petty quarrel (4)

Solution see page 240

33

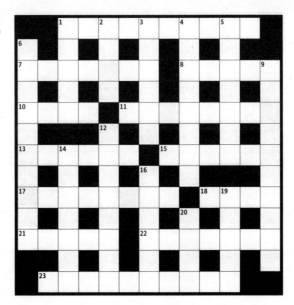

ACROSS

1 Lowest possible level (4,6)
7 Harry Potter author (7)
8 Trimmed — peeled (5)
10 River over which Charon carried dead souls (4)
11 Exceptional (8)
13 Best ever performance (6)
15 Pleasant smells (6)
17 Snow storm (8)
18 Trounce (4)
21 Exhaust (5)
22 Large Arctic deer (7)
23 Officials who once made public announcements (4,6)

DOWN

1 Loud and rough (5)
2 Gambling token (4)
3 Away with you! (6)
4 First-rate (3-5)
5 Rower (7)
6 Forbidden (10)
9 Salted and strongly flavoured cheese (6,4)
12 Person from Phoenix? (8)
14 The Windy City (7)
16 Investigator looking for missing person(s) (6)
19 Flowing outer garments (5)
20 Faithful (4)

Solution see page 241

34

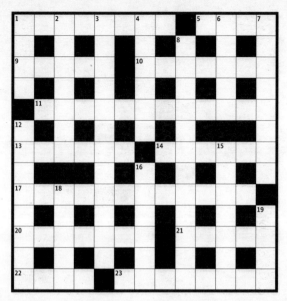

ACROSS

1 Eccentrics (8)
5 Careless mistake (4)
9 Wailing alarm (5)
10 Long pillow (7)
11 You can't get colder than this (8,4)
13 Long narrow depression in the ocean bed (6)
14 Dies down (6)
17 Determination despite setbacks (12)
20 Abdominal organs (7)
21 Not seriously (2,3)
22 Impetuous (4)
23 Land-locked east Asian country (8)

DOWN

1 City 1,400 miles east of Moscow on the Trans-Siberian Railway (4)
2 Long lasting (7)
3 Henry VIII's fourth wife (4,2,6)
4 Childbirth (6)
6 Espresso with steamed milk (5)
7 Marine mammal (8)
8 Encompassing everything (3-9)
12 Break in a journey (8)
15 Diplomatic (7)
16 (Musically) the opposite of staccato (6)
18 Hybrid tea, floribunda etc (5)
19 Old Andean (4)

Solution see page 241

35

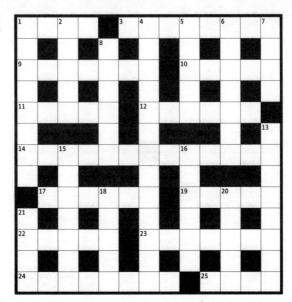

ACROSS

1 Persuade gently (4)
3 Sheath for a sword (8)
9 Et cetera (3,2,2)
10 Layabout (5)
11 Beguiled unwisely (3,2)
12 Image of a person (6)
14 Immediate (13)
17 Affair (anag) — mat-making fibre (6)
19 Most populous city in the United Arab Emirates (5)
22 Bring up (5)
23 Leading (2,5)
24 Not varying in pitch (8)
25 Single-storey storage building (4)

DOWN

1 Padre (8)
2 Increased (5)
4 Close attention (13)
5 Concise (5)
6 (Musically) quick and lively (7)
7 Scottish dagger (4)
8 Balkan country, capital Sarajevo (6)
13 Aided (8)
15 Pacific marine mammal (3,4)
16 Fall asleep (3,3)
18 Fast (5)
20 Thin soup (5)
21 Public transport vehicle (4)

Solution see page 241

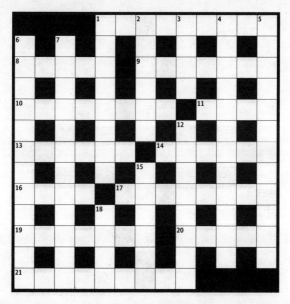

ACROSS

1 Tuneful (9)
8 Decorate (5)
9 Italian dumplings (7)
10 Faithfulness (8)
11 Court card (4)
13 List of corrections in published material (6)
14 Salt used in fertilisers — hot spa (anag) (6)
16 Tardy (4)
17 Agra's main tourist attraction (3,5)
19 Let go (7)
20 Greek letter (5)
21 Prohibition-era barroom (9)

DOWN

1 Standing stone (8)
2 Illuminations (6)
3 Means of ingress or egress (4)
4 Now and then (4,2,1,5)
5 Shirk work (5,3,4)
6 Actions that are not forceful enough (4,8)
7 Type of sheepdog (6,6)
12 End of the world? (8)
15 A single-lens reflex, for example (6)
18 Peddle from place to place (4)

Solution see page 241

37

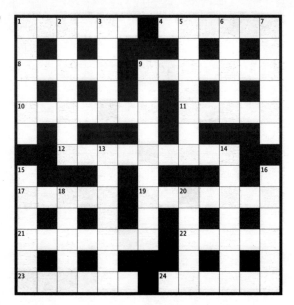

ACROSS

1 Exactly right (4,2)
4 Accessories (3-3)
8 Extremely angry (5)
9 Bodily structure (7)
10 Fierce fish (7)
11 Circumference (5)
12 French philosopher, d. 1650 (9)
17 Subsequently (5)
19 Attire (7)
21 Distance travelled (7)
22 Muslim jurist — civvies (5)
23 Stop (6)
24 Indian fig tree (6)

DOWN

1 Dilapidated old car (6)
2 Cut off (7)
3 East African country (5)
5 Current of air (7)
6 Nasty smell (5)
7 Hand-held reaping tool (6)
9 Overwhelming influx (9)
13 Outdo (7)
14 Tipsy (7)
15 Made less cold (6)
16 Great in number (6)
18 Ankle bone (5)
20 Polynesian country, capital Apia (5)

Solution see page 242

38

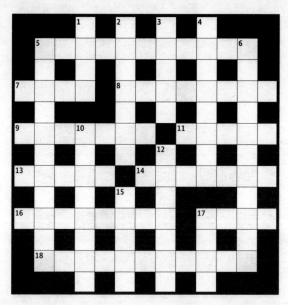

ACROSS

5 Annual literary award (6,5)
7 Berkshire college for boys, founded 1440 (4)
8 Happy-go-lucky (8)
9 Voted into office (7)
11 Banal (5)
13 Attach (5)
14 Being tested (2,5)
16 Figure of speech (8)
17 Enter (2,2)
18 Taking pleasure in doing dangerous things (11)

DOWN

1 Lewd printed or visual material (abbr) (4)
2 Freed — seducer (anag) (7)
3 Hurling, curling etc (5)
4 Petty thief (8)
5 Scene of military action (11)
6 Possible outcome (11)
10 Courteous behaviour (8)
12 Avenger (anag) — chase (7)
15 Rebuke (5)
17 Force 8 on the Beaufort scale (4)

Solution see page 242

39

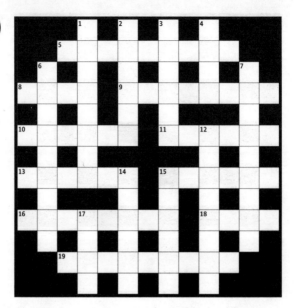

ACROSS

5 Make visual signals — a posher me (anag) (9)

8 Warty amphibian (4)

9 Building divided into let flats (8)

10 Arboreal ape — English historian, d. 1794 (6)

11 Hire — engage (6)

13 Small savoury dumplings (3,3)

15 Small room for storing food (6)

16 (Of metal) with an oxide coating (8)

18 Toast holder? (4)

19 Where the French Lieutenant's Woman lived on the Dorset coast (4,5)

DOWN

1 Articulated passenger vehicle (5,3)

2 Patterned cloth associated with a Scottish clan (6)

3 Opportunity (6)

4 Baby carriage (4)

6 French territory bought by the United States in 1803 for $15m (9)

7 Freedom from guilt (9)

12 Depiction of a person (8)

14 Original recording from which copies can be made (6)

15 Person renting accommodation in someone's house (6)

17 24-hour periods (4)

Solution see page 242

40

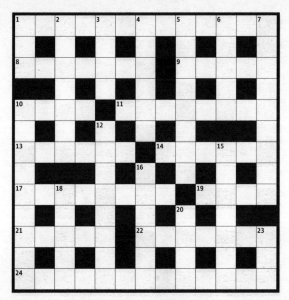

ACROSS

1 Citrus fruit — overseeing all (anag) (7,6)

8 Royal residences (7)

9 Sworn promises (5)

10 US vagrant (4)

11 Salad of shredded cabbage etc (8)

13 Required (6)

14 Pacific atoll, used for 23 US nuclear tests between 1946 and 1958 (6)

17 In foreign parts (8)

19 Highest point of achievement (4)

21 Large milk container (5)

22 Ways and means (7)

24 American jazz singer, d, 1959 (6,7)

DOWN

1 Plant juice (3)

2 Fluent in speech (7)

3 Deficiency (4)

4 London rail terminus (6)

5 Zimbabwe's former name (8)

6 Birth-related (5)

7 Former (9)

10 Victorian mode of transport (6,3)

12 Nordic capital (8)

15 Those in the know? (2–5)

16 Affection (6)

18 Peer (5)

20 And elsewhere (abbr) (2,2)

23 Utter (3)

Solution see page 242

41

ACROSS

1 Chirping insect (6)

4 Italian island where Gracie Fields lived for the last part of her life (5)

7 Fruit in a tarte Tatin (6)

8 Event that is not repeated (3-3)

9 Fly high (4)

10 Large shop (8)

12 Goodbye for now (3,3,5)

17 Underwater swimmer (8)

19 Lady singer, b. 1986 (4)

20 Underground passage (6)

21 Kind of beer (6)

22 Assorted (5)

23 Written (6)

DOWN

1 Plentiful (7)

2 Unit of heat energy (7)

3 Othello's wife (9)

4 Africa's second longest river (5)

5 Supply (7)

6 Notoriety (6)

11 Tasty (9)

13 Annual moments when day and night both last about 12 hours everywhere (7)

14 Screw up (7)

15 Plant of the daisy family — Edgware (anag) (7)

16 Large metal gong (3-3)

18 Very much (informal) (2,3)

Solution see page 243

42

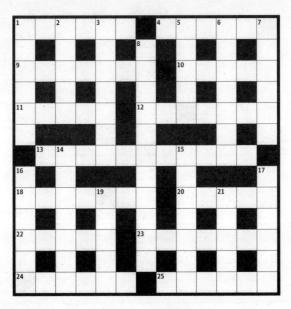

ACROSS

1 Endorse (6)
4 Not open to the public (6)
9 Peach juice and champagne cocktail (7)
10 Ship of the desert (5)
11 Pinch sharply (5)
12 Briefly (2,5)
13 Very successful recording (5-6)
18 (In horse racing) the smallest possible margin of victory (2,1,4)
20 Long-barrelled firearm (5)
22 Long films (5)
23 Region disputed between India and Pakistan since 1947 (7)
24 Garment worn by dancers (6)
25 Winter slider (6)

DOWN

1 Deduction or discount (6)
2 Mark used over 'a' or 'o' in Portuguese (5)
3 Glimmer (7)
5 Scene of an event (5)
6 Talk cosily (7)
7 Water down (6)
8 Just a dream! (3,2,3,3)
14 Aural sense (7)
15 Reading (7)
16 Express disapproval (6)
17 Grade (6)
19 Early stage (5)
21 Well-known (5)

Solution see page 243

43

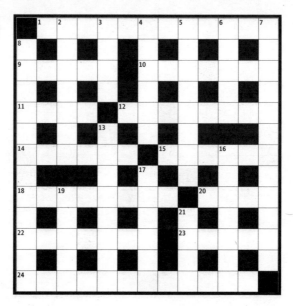

ACROSS

1 Sound of a horse trotting (8–4)

9 Arctic natives (5)

10 Landlocked country with joint heads of state, the president of France and the bishop of Urgell (7)

11 Swirl (4)

12 From a noble family (4–4)

14 Middle East country, established 1948 (6)

15 Thin covering over wood (6)

18 Flowering shrub or tree — burn alum (anag) (8)

20 In vogue (4)

22 Africa country that won independence from Ethiopia in 1993 (7)

23 Rough and ready (5)

24 Where mislaid items await retrieval (4,8)

DOWN

2 Wash (7)

3 Seasoned meat or fish spread (4)

4 In high spirits (6)

5 Swiss mountain songster? (8)

6 (Musically) slow and dignified (5)

7 South-east Asian snack food (5,7)

8 We'll see! (4,4,4)

13 Salty liquid bead (8)

16 Tire out (7)

17 (Musically) with a flexible tempo — BA tour (anag) (6)

19 Seventh heaven (5)

21 4,840 square yards (4)

Solution see page 243

44

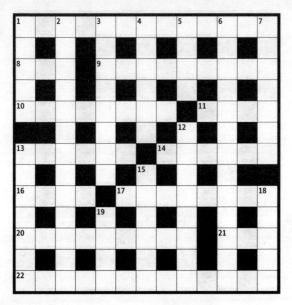

ACROSS

1 Barney (8,5)
8 Indian state, with Vasco da Gama its largest city (3)
9 Beautiful young Greek who fell in love with his own reflection (9)
10 Elevenses? (3,5)
11 Short tail, eg of a deer (4)
13 Deposit sticking to teeth (6)
14 Twine (6)
16 Some (1,3)
17 Laid low (8)
20 Consequently (9)
21 Get brown (3)
22 Entire river basin (9,4)

DOWN

1 Seeing faculty (5)
2 600-mile arid plateau of northern Chile (7,6)
3 Large (8)
4 Nothing special (6)
5 Cripple (4)
6 International bowler, for example (4,9)
7 Word prefaced by # used for online cross-referencing (7)
12 Raucous (8)
13 Easily moulded (7)
15 Caress with the hands (6)
18 Mercenary or covert agent in feudal Japan (5)
19 Interlock (4)

Solution see page 243

45

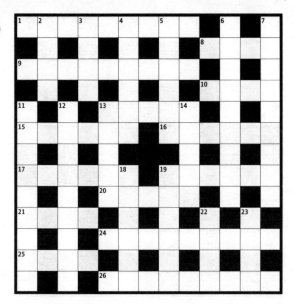

ACROSS

1 Church residence (9)
8 Small inlet (4)
9 Folklore story (5,4)
10 Small sturdy four-wheel-drive vehicle (4)
13 Sailing boat with one mast (5)
15 Mum's sis? (6)
16 North Atlantic flatfish (6)
17 Sound made by a small petrol engine (3-3)
19 Last part of a performance (6)
20 New branch (5)
21 Musical based on TS Eliot poems (4)
24 Small enclosed space (9)
25 Food (sometimes small) (4)
26 Card game — set up dork (anag) (4,5)

DOWN

2 Man of Eden (4)
3 Shore breakers (4)
4 Annoy — stinger (6)
5 Fast equine pace (6)
6 American author of Myra Breckinridge. d. 2012 (4,5)
7 Puzzled (9)
11 Extremely crowded (3-6)
12 Association for the promotion of art, science or education (9)
13 Passage connecting to nasal cavities (5)
14 Hair style created by braiding (5)
18 Shove (6)
19 Veto (6)
22 Be off with you! (4)
23 Gum (4)

Solution see page 244

46

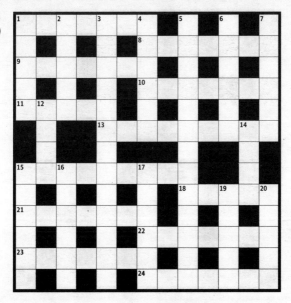

ACROSS

1 Gear (7)
8 Holidaymaker (7)
9 Paper-based art form (7)
10 Without payment (3,4)
11 That place (5)
13 Whatever the reason, it must not happen! (2,7)
15 Third of 51 (9)
18 Overhanging part of roof (5)
21 Fishy girl? (7)
22 Bring to mind (7)
23 Add sugar (7)
24 Time between school and uni? (3,4)

DOWN

1 Native of Split, perhaps (5)
2 Black or green stoned fruit (5)
3 A perfect situation? (6,2,5)
4 Smother (6)
5 Oil-fired light — numerical harp (anag) (9,4)
6 Fruit with a thick rind and juicy edible pulp inside (6)
7 Emphasise (6)
12 Ginormous (4)
14 Lip (4)
15 In Indian cooking, a small fried turnover filled with vegetables or meat (6)
16 Whirlpool (6)
17 Last part (6)
19 Articulate (5)
20 Promise (5)

Solution see page 244

47

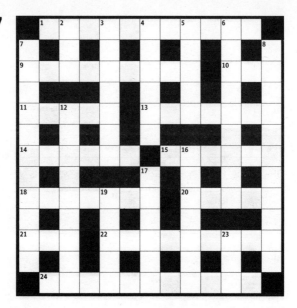

ACROSS

1 Beautiful young woman (7,4)
9 Indefensible (9)
10 Since (3)
11 Loathe (5)
13 Summer drink (4,3)
14 Hanging down (6)
15 Fly (6)
18 Useful feature — any time (anag) (7)
20 Jog (5)
21 Tail (3)
22 Unaccompanied liturgical chant (9)
24 The box (5,6)

DOWN

2 On fire (3)
3 Poacher catcher (7)
4 Italian region, capital Perugia (6)
5 Irritate (5)
6 Rectangular piece of plastic holding personal data required for financial transactions (5,4)
7 Shenanigans — nudge ma's fan (anag) (3,3,5)
8 Natural source of electrical power (5,6)
12 Colorado River barrier in Nevada, constructed in the 1930s (6,3)
16 Wine merchant (7)
17 Regulations made by a local authority (6)
19 Force (5)
23 Bravo in Barcelona? (3)

Solution see page 244

48

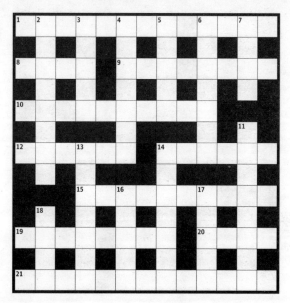

ACROSS

1 Enchantress who gave King Arthur his sword, Excalibur (4,2,3,4)
8 St Paul's Cathedral architect (4)
9 Transport systems with carriers suspended from cables supported by towers (8)
10 Primary storey (5,5)
12 Tough and spirited (6)
14 Cricket's appeal (6)
15 Barrel organ played by cranking a wheel (5–5)
19 Nineteenth-century British PM (8)
20 Decisive point (4)
21 Undress completely (3,4,3,3)

DOWN

2 Redeemable points earned by flying (3,5)
3 Years and years (5)
4 Glowing beetle (7)
5 River horse (abbr) (5)
6 Not for intellectuals? (7)
7 Knockout (4)
11 Bits off the scalp (8)
13 (Musically) a playful movement (7)
14 Stack of dried grass (7)
16 Female ruff (5)
17 Not abridged (5)
18 Narrow — excellent (4)

49

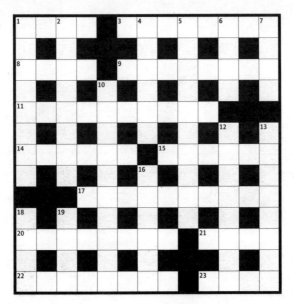

ACROSS

1 Patient — legal action (4)
3 Wind-eroded dry area of the United States (4,4)
8 Threaten (4)
9 Excessively instructive (8)
11 Give up (10)
14 Reject (6)
15 Smoked breakfast fish (6)
17 Novelty show with insects (4,6)
20 Speech (8)
21 Extinct bird of Mauritius (4)
22 Bad behaviour (8)
23 That seems unlikely! (2,2)

DOWN

1 Kind of beetle, a potato pest (8)
2 Perfectly clean (8)
4 Singular (6)
5 Willingness to work together (4,6)
6 Obscene word or expression (4)
7 Wingless bloodsuckers (4)
10 Machine for clearing flakes? (10)
12 Convincing at first, but flawed (8)
13 Rebuff (5,3)
16 Rinse throat with mouthwash (6)
18 (Of probability) remote (4)
19 Responsibility (4)

Solution see page 245

50

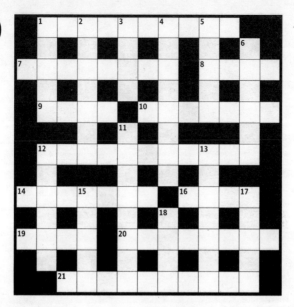

ACROSS

1 Excellent gag (3-7)

7 Person who remains doubtful (8)

8 Delight (4)

9 System of exercises to promote control of body and mind (4)

10 Lack (of) (7)

12 Happy-go-lucky — a rum car hums (anag) (5-6)

14 Fickle (7)

16 Lacking sensation (4)

19 Pulse (4)

20 Party acting game (8)

21 Over fastidious (10)

DOWN

1 Game where forward passes are illegal (5)

2 Internet commentator (7)

3 Taking lively interest in (4)

4 Bribe (8)

5 Bird of prey with broad wings (5)

6 Digital filming device for putting images on the internet (6)

11 Symbol expressing feelings — to come in (anag) (8)

12 Shout out loudly (informal) (6)

13 Food cooked or served in a roll (7)

15 Bottled spirit? (5)

17 Smelling of bitter? (5)

18 Of those who aren't clergy (4)

Solution see page 245

51

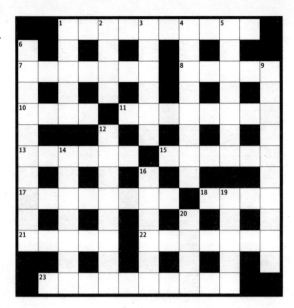

ACROSS

1 Hedgerow plant — osprey claw (anag) (3,7)
7 Piece of jewellery (7)
8 Blackfly or greenfly? (5)
10 Judge (4)
11 Vivid red (8)
13 Bionic man (Victor Stone) (6)
15 Wheel-and-rope device for lifting things (6)
17 Sometimes (2,3,3)
18 Festival (4)
21 Informal language (5)
22 Red or white butterfly (7)
23 Pirate flag (5,5)

DOWN

1 Swear (5)
2 Caprice (4)
3 Sea between Greece and Turkey (6)
4 Be prominent (5,3)
5 Colourless constituent of alcoholic drinks — not hale (anag) (7)
6 Intentionally untrue (10)
9 Dawdle (5-5)
12 Spendthrift (8)
14 Showing-off (7)
16 Matter of some concern (6)
19 Drier (5)
20 Atmospheric pollutant (4)

Solution see page 245

52

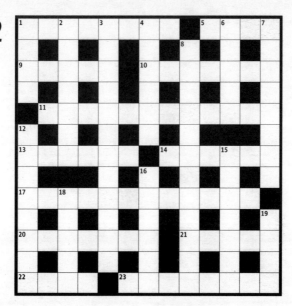

ACROSS

1 Future moment of financial need (5,3)

5 Move by steps and hops (4)

9 Au revoir (5)

10 Campaigning movement (7)

11 Current champions in the Bundesliga (6,6)

13 Devon city, founded by the Romans as Isca in the first century AD (6)

14 Gabled extension built out from a sloping roof (6)

17 Good gracious me! (6,1,5)

20 Solidified from molten volcanic material (7)

21 Bungle (5)

22 Spanish romantic painter, d. 1828 (4)

23 Enter without permission (8)

DOWN

1 Harvest (4)

2 Copy (7)

3 It could happen! (3,5,4)

4 Brogue (6)

6 Sturdy twill used for army uniforms (5)

7 Abundance — help rota (anag) (8)

8 Towering vertical storm cloud (12)

12 Pain inflicted by a small winged insect (3,5)

15 Holy Brahmin sage (7)

16 Thick nautical rope or cable (6)

18 Fluid (5)

19 The item here (4)

Solution see page 245

53

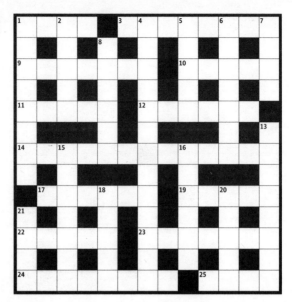

ACROSS

1 Soothing ointment (4)
3 Angelic (8)
9 Bogeyman (7)
10 Stimulate curiosity (5)
11 Rudimentary (5)
12 Ship's smokestack (6)
14 Portable engine for a boat (8,5)
17 Crisps, sandwiches etc (6)
19 Eat as much as you like! (3,2)
22 Short ad (5)
23 Awaiting resolution (2,5)
24 On the payroll (8)
25 Floating structure like Thor Heyerdahl's Kon–Tiki (4)

DOWN

1 Significant increase in the birth rate (4,4)
2 Racing sleds (5)
4 Watford is the largest town in this Home County (13)
5 Mature (5)
6 Legacy (7)
7 Team in charge of an aeroplane (4)
8 Fastener — clover (anag) (6)
13 Page(s) run off from a computer (8)
15 Food wrapping made of aluminium (7)
16 Confuse (6)
18 Singing group (5)
20 Greek equivalent of G (5)
21 Musical work (4)

Solution see page 246

54

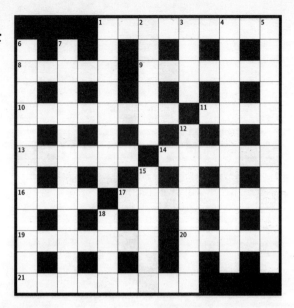

ACROSS

1 Wine bottle opener (9)
8 Place where something happens (5)
9 Portable rocket launcher (7)
10 Two half hitches tied to fasten cords together securely (4,4)
11 Femur or fibula, for example (4)
13 Secure against (6)
14 Cling (6)
16 Obscure (4)
17 Give courage (8)
19 Brilliant and showy skill in performing (7)
20 Language spoken by Sitting Bull and his Dakota people (5)
21 English plotter against James I, remembered on 5 November (3,6)

DOWN

1 Squeaky sound — cake ring (anag) (8)
2 Load a computer's starting program again (6)
3 Magnitude (4)
4 Evergreen shrub with leathery leaves and bell-shaped flowers (12)
5 Expression of amazement (8,4)
6 Case packed for short stay (9,3)
7 Go-between (12)
12 Leading singers — toss s oil (anag) (8)
15 Get on board (6)
18 Atmosphere surrounding something (4)

Solution see page 246

55

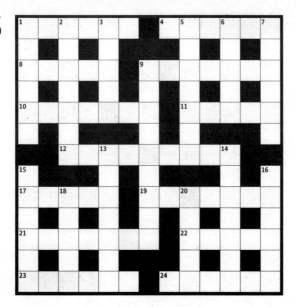

ACROSS

1 Muscle that flexes a forearm (6)
4 Phantom (6)
8 Talk pompously (5)
9 Selected candidate (7)
10 Develop very promisingly (7)
11 Lovers' secret meeting (5)
12 Effigy for frightening off birds (9)
17 Thoroughbred horses (5)
19 Stone pillar with a rectangular cross section tapering upwards (7)
21 Neologism (7)
22 Tropical fruit with orange flesh and small black seeds (5)
23 Stucco-like substance applied to masonry (6)
24 Edible body of a marine mollusc (6)

DOWN

1 Splotched (6)
2 Soft sheepskin suede (7)
3 Media (5)
5 Pet rodent (7)
6 Very good — British comic (5)
7 Circular arrangement of foliage or flowers (6)
9 Chart-topping hit — myself (6,3)
13 Up for grabs (2,5)
14 Small greyhound cross, bred for racing (7)
15 Sign of the zodiac (6)
16 Transfix (6)
18 Foreign (5)
20 Void (5)

Solution see page 246

56

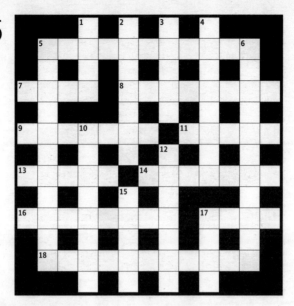

ACROSS

5 Country steps for four couples (6,5)
7 Kiss and cuddle (informal) (4)
8 Menace (8)
9 Marvellous chap (4,3)
11 Nice view (5)
13 Robinson Crusoe author (5)
14 Where clothes get washed and ironed (7)
16 I'm amazed! (2,6)
17 Plates of meat? (4)
18 In difficulty (2,7,2)

DOWN

1 Shelf-like berth (4)
2 One guided by some older person (7)
3 Deck out (5)
4 Encroachment (8)
5 1963 Beatles hit (3,5,3)
6 Device for throwing a pilot from the cockpit (7,4)
10 Of a bishopric (8)
12 Hot pepper (7)
15 Die (like a frog?) (5)
17 Lot — fortune (4)

Solution see page 246

57

ACROSS

5 Appeal of play or film as judged by ticket sales (3,6)
8 Secular form of gospel music (4)
9 Insurrection (8)
10 Hard magnetic metal, Co (6)
11 Good-oh! (6)
13 Naughty (6)
15 Fuzzy (6)
16 Intuitive reaction (8)
18 Woof (4)
19 Closely resembling (9)

DOWN

1 Variety of cabbage with edible leaves and turnip-like stem (8)
2 Grasshopper, cause of one of the Ten Plagues of Egypt (6)
3 Noisy altercation (6)
4 Serves that the receiver can't even reach (4)
6 Please don't! — May I? (2,3,4)
7 Facing attack (5,4)
12 System of pipes (8)
14 Famished (6)
15 Time from now onward (6)
17 Hard labour (4)

Solution see page 247

58

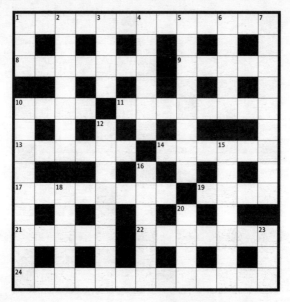

ACROSS

1 Transport for the 9-to-5 brigade? (8,5)

8 In the style of an English romantic poet, d. 1824 (7)

9 Form of address for a woman (5)

10 Society — card (4)

11 Caviar fish (8)

13 Upshot (6)

14 Open by drawing back the bar (6)

17 Unexpected (8)

19 Cow group (4)

21 Load for shipment (5)

22 Collection of diverse things (7)

24 Wise partner? (4,9)

DOWN

1 Small round loaf — male swan (3)

2 French nobleman like de Sade (7)

3 Arm bone (4)

4 Stimulate (6)

5 Large evergreen tropical tree — darn it, Ma! (anag) (8)

6 Become rotten (5)

7 Chosen (9)

10 Infection larger than a boil (9)

12 Grub-like wingless female beetle with luminous organs (4-4)

15 How one bowls? (7)

16 Restorative drink (6)

18 Bones of the ankle and foot — sitar (anag) (5)

20 Group of politicians with common objectives? (4)

23 The day before (3)

Solution see page 247

59

ACROSS

1 Coney (6)

4 Elegant and fashionable (5)

7 Hindu festival with lights, celebrating the end of the monsoon (6)

8 Not divisible by two (6)

9 Energetic dance — swing music (4)

10 Plant with large brightly coloured flowers — cub is his (anag) (8)

12 Consonant formed in Estuary English, making 'butter' sound as 'bu/er' — plot lost tag (anag) (7,4)

17 Galaxy (5,3)

19 Holy Father (4)

20 Mountain peak where Noah's Ark landed (6)

21 Person who plunders (6)

22 Attempt to pull a fast one (3–2)

23 Indifference to life (6)

DOWN

1 Barrier consisting of bars (7)

2 Mexican agricultural labourer in the US — crab roe (anag) (7)

3 Hibernian meat and veg dish (5,4)

4 One of the two main branches of orthodox Islam (5)

5 Without reference to anything else (Latin) (2,5)

6 Frank and reliable (6)

11 Ungainly (and painful) dive (5,4)

13 Song for bedtime (7)

14 Main support for a tree, growing straight downward from the trunk (7)

15 Hot (7)

16 Diacritical mark used in German (ä, ö, ü) (6)

18 Hanker (5)

Solution see page 247

60

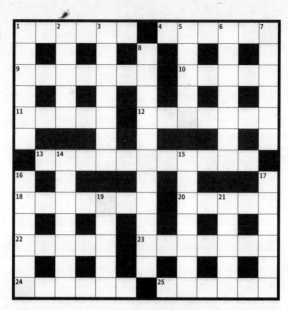

ACROSS

1 Draw (while thinking about other things?) (6)
4 Fight (6)
9 Alchemist's universal remedy (7)
10 Ground and sifted meal (5)
11 (Cause to) bend (5)
12 Fun involving singing to a backing track (7)
13 No-nonsense (4,2,5)
18 Open air (7)
20 Cups and saucers — cockney friend (5)
22 Obscure (5)
23 Pot of savings (4,3)
24 ____ Waugh, Decline and Fall author (6)
25 Twist and turn (6)

DOWN

1 Portray (6)
2 Proprietor (5)
3 Support for a speaker? (7)
5 Bid (5)
6 Lavish meal (4-3)
7 Small tower (6)
8 Wrong way round (4,2,5)
14 Conclusion (7)
15 One who points the finger (7)
16 That hit home! (6)
17 (Make a) metallic sound (6)
19 In a strange way (5)
21 Torpid (5)

Solution see page 247

61

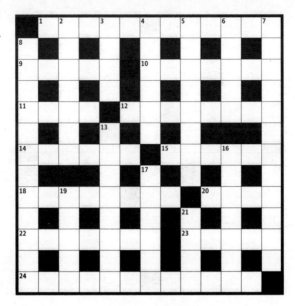

ACROSS

1 Soldiers who lead the way (7,5)
9 Manner of speaking (5)
10 Spin (7)
11 Follow (4)
12 Sam loses (anag) — thick dark syrup (8)
14 Sorrow (6)
15 Holmes's doctor friend (6)
18 Listeners — spectators (8)
20 Joker? (4)
22 Open-minded (7)
23 Twankey's social status? (5)
24 Old slide projector (5,7)

DOWN

2 Vigorous (7)
3 Plans (4)
4 Cardboard container (6)
5 Unfortunate disclosure (8)
6 Map book (5)
7 Severe telling-off (8-4)
8 Stoned fruit (8,4)
13 Dazzling — quick (8)
16 Defame (7)
17 Greek sea monster who devoured sailors (6)
19 Detect and remove secret microphones (5)
21 Studious type (4)

Solution see page 248

62

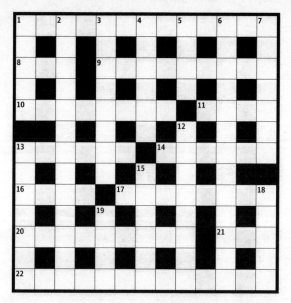

ACROSS

1 Impartial (13)
8 Greek letter X, equivalent to Ch in English (3)
9 Form a mental picture (9)
10 Renounce (8)
11 Bloodsucking insect (4)
13 Reason (6)
14 Complain in an annoying way (6)
16 Latest information (4)
17 Caution (8)
20 Deficit in bank account (9)
21 Split (3)
22 Shaw's Major Barbara wore its uniform (9,4)

DOWN

1 Russian holiday home (5)
2 Old machine for making yarn (8,5)
3 Steer (8)
4 Imitation (6)
5 Flair (4)
6 Experimental way to find what works (5,3,5)
7 When to expect a new arrival (3,4)
12 Name (8)
13 Serpentine (7)
15 Seasoned sausage for slicing (6)
18 Sentimental (5)
19 Thought (4)

Solution see page 248

63

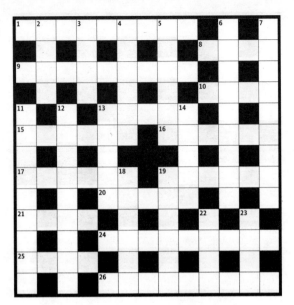

ACROSS

1 Wind-up mechanism (9)
8 Surge (4)
9 Using compressed air (9)
10 Online journal (4)
13 Soft round brimless hat (5)
15 Scallywag (6)
16 St George's adversary (6)
17 A large quantity (6)
19 He'll lock up (6)
20 Sturdy (5)
21 Regulation — measure (4)
24 Forecast (9)
25 Nonsense (4)
26 So it's claimed (9)

DOWN

2 Extended (4)
3 Close friend (4)
4 Sneaky person (6)
5 Damaged beyond repair (6)
6 Iron pyrite (5,4)
7 Fictitious (9)
11 Recommend as beneficial (9)
12 Alsatians (anag) — aggressor (9)
13 Luxuriates (5)
14 Step (5)
18 Plant with leaves used in salads and cookery — reddish-brown horse (6)
19 Catchy promotional tune or song (6)
22 Drug — information (4)
23 List of performers (4)

Solution see page 248

64

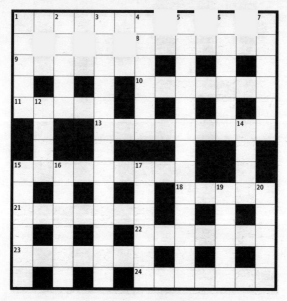

ACROSS

1 Hottest time of the year (3,4)
8 Small-time criminal (7)
9 Fast ball bowled aggressively short (7)
10 One in the know (7)
11 The ___ Man, 1949 film about Harry Lime (5)
13 Vacancy (9)
15 Intermediary (2–7)
18 Stealing (5)
21 Initially (2,5)
22 Joy or hate, for example (7)
23 Knot of hair arranged at the back of the head (7)
24 Hanging decorations of threads gathered at the top (7)

DOWN

1 Payment still owed (5)
2 Spanish architect, greatest exponent of Catalan Modernism, d. 1926 (5)
3 Often involved in mishaps — it concerned PA (anag) (8–5)
4 Basis of a seafood cocktail? (6)
5 Painstaking (13)
6 Commit(ment) (6)
7 Hurts (6)
12 Visible indication of holiness (4)
14 Ego (4)
15 Hit at an angle and bounce off (6)
16 Egghead (6)
17 Full distance (6)
19 Enforced absence (5)
20 Chinese secret organisations (5)

Solution see page 248

65

ACROSS

1 Good times and bad times (3,3,5)
9 Too early (9)
10 Sticky stuff (3)
11 Neat (informal) (5)
13 Grid-type structure (7)
14 Bricklayer's tool (6)
15 Claim (6)
18 Ludicrous (7)
20 Room at the top (5)
21 Contagious viral infection (3)
22 No longer necessary (9)
24 Not made to order (3-3-5)

DOWN

2 Pastry dish (3)
3 Closely inspect (7)
4 Twice (6)
5 Blatant (5)
6 Failing to take proper care (9)
7 Prodigal (11)
8 Tame (11)
12 Something to eat (9)
16 Unswerving (7)
17 Irritate (6)
19 Break apart (5)
23 Everyone (3)

Solution see page 249

66

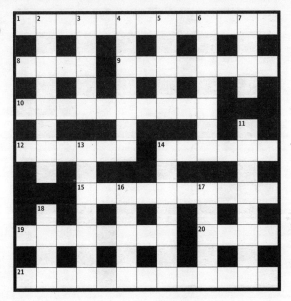

ACROSS

1 Furtive — Tories' pursuit (anag) (13)
8 Dubious (informal) (4)
9 Basic — unadorned (2-6)
10 Unconventional individual (4,6)
12 To an intense degree (6)
14 Memory (6)
15 Lustful (10)
19 First and last (5,3)
20 Similar (4)
21 Where to begin? (8,5)

DOWN

2 Amorphous (8)
3 Verse (5)
4 Range (7)
5 Conclude (5)
6 Very silly (7)
7 Unattractive (4)
11 Fantasy (8)
13 Rigmarole (7)
14 Warning sign (3,4)
16 Indian snack of vegetables in batter (5)
17 ___ Marsh, New Zealand crime writer, d. 1982 (5)
18 Border (4)

Solution see page 249

67

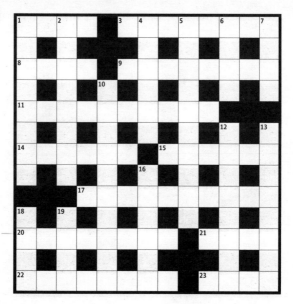

ACROSS

1 Hope (4)
3 Brought to an abrupt conclusion (3,5)
8 One-sided win (4)
9 Against the current (8)
11 Painful condition of the joints and muscles (10)
14 Show anger (6)
15 Lacking foresight (6)
17 On the streets (4-3-3)
20 Mimic (8)
21 Platform sticking out into the water (4)
22 Threadbare (8)
23 Give over (4)

DOWN

1 Clothing collection (8)
2 Holiday reminder (8)
4 Self-important (6)
5 Meeting a need (10)
6 Toe the line (4)
7 Casual worker (4)
10 Improve (10)
12 Contrary (8)
13 Without penalty (4-4)
16 Enamoured (2,4)
18 One of two British prime ministers (4)
19 General idea (4)

Solution see page 249

68

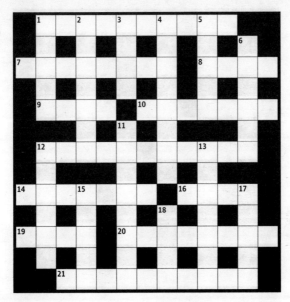

ACROSS

1 Out of trouble (3,3,4)
7 Predator (8)
8 Spill the beans (4)
9 Space (4)
10 Eggs Florentine ingredient (7)
12 Tempted hero (anag) — easily provoked (3-8)
14 Popular saying (7)
16 Employs (4)
19 Make unclear (4)
20 Underprivileged (8)
21 Using it's a grind (6,4)

DOWN

1 Being broadcast (2,3)
2 Lying in a state of total exhaustion (4,3)
3 Covered structure from which to observe birds (4)
4 Sailors's jig (8)
5 Many times (5)
6 Calm (6)
11 Equipped and ready to go (6,2)
12 Signal (6)
13 Composer of The Barber of Seville, d. 1868 (7)
15 Energetic style (5)
17 Hard outer covering (5)
18 Encouragement (4)

Solution see page 249

69

ACROSS

1 Fortune-hunter (4-6)
7 Blue, carpet or gulf (7)
8 Short sharp fight (3-2)
10 Vessel with handle and spout (4)
11 Activist (8)
13 Come about (6)
15 Recurring sound pattern (6)
17 Very large (8)
18 Legislation (4)
21 Descendant (5)
22 1971 Elstree comedy film — Up ___ (7)
23 See dollars (anag) — not-for-profit item for sale (4,6)

DOWN

1 Eat like a pig (5)
2 Wild animal's abode (4)
3 Hopper, Nilsen or Potter? (6)
4 Manipulate someone psychologically into thinking that they are mad (8)
5 Pull out (7)
6 Stunned into silence (10)
9 Like Pollyanna? (10)
12 Something sailors (and others) don't want to be on (4-4)
14 Condition (7)
16 Flexible (6)
19 Obvious (5)
20 Surrounded by (4)

Solution see page 250

70

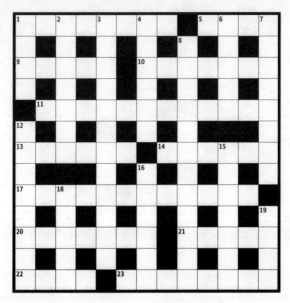

ACROSS

1 Traitor (8)
5 Way through the mountains (4)
9 Like a Roman Catholic bull? (5)
10 Outline (7)
11 Someone who gets tied up at work? (12)
13 Bible reading in church service (6)
14 Alternative (6)
17 Good works (12)
20 Mutual understanding (7)
21 US electric car maker (5)
22 Core (4)
23 Critical trial (4,4)

DOWN

1 Outstrips (4)
2 Rests (7)
3 Partner (in crime, perhaps) (12)
4 Secure — TV presenter (6)
6 Mediterranean garlic-flavoured sauce (5)
7 Close examination (8)
8 Unified — coriander pot (anag) (12)
12 Nonsense (8)
15 Dead end (7)
16 Interference with radio or TV (6)
18 Comment or statement that adds information (5)
19 Devon river (4)

Solution see page 250

71

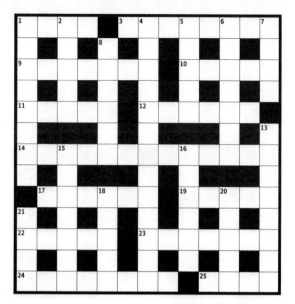

ACROSS

1 Very small distance to lose a horse race by (4)

3 Prison boss (8)

9 Mundane (7)

10 Morning (or evening) star (5)

11 Conditions (5)

12 All that one owns (6)

14 Seasoning combination (4,3,6)

17 Decorative plaster (6)

19 Temporary business venture (3-2)

22 Lifting equipment (5)

23 Flavoursome little fish, often salted, used for hors d'oeuvres or in sauces (7)

24 Voyeur's vantage point (8)

25 Eve's third son (4)

DOWN

1 Giving friends or family preferential treatment (8)

2 Trail left behind by an animal (5)

4 Conclusively (4,3,3,3)

5 He has left the building (5)

6 Unending (3-4)

7 Sudden burst of activity (4)

8 Sick feeling (6)

13 Artwork in three parts (8)

15 The army's convenience? (7)

16 Await (6)

18 Angler's haul (5)

20 Inclined (5)

21 Parliamentary enforcer (4)

Solution see page 250

72

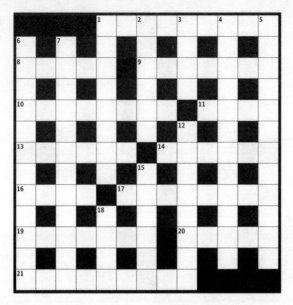

ACROSS

1 It promised but finally disappointed (4,5)

8 Demolish — flatten (5)

9 Social no-no (4,3)

10 Vauxhall or Volkswagen? (3,5)

11 Smile (4)

13 Place for keeping personal belongings (6)

14 Area of hard skin (6)

16 Insubstantial (4)

17 In a confused rush (4-4)

19 Wrap completely (7)

20 Edible sea snail (5)

21 Fought (9)

DOWN

1 Stuffed vine leaves (8)

2 Offended (informal) (6)

3 Not sweet (4)

4 With no equals — lead Prunella! (anag) (12)

5 Professional (12)

6 Capital writing style (5,7)

7 One who gets further than expected (12)

12 Sacred (8)

15 Friendly American correspondent (3,3)

18 Gulp of strong drink (4)

Solution see page 250

73

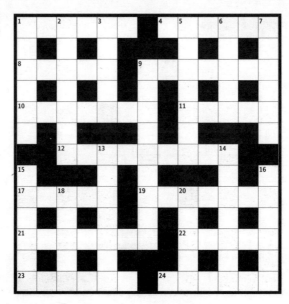

ACROSS

1 Stock (6)
4 Zany (6)
8 Delight in (5)
9 Aha, a pro! (anag) — a Native American (7)
10 Bone of the upper arm (7)
11 Professional representative (5)
12 Extremely famous player (9)
17 Paved garden area (5)
19 Large edible marine gastropod (7)
21 Subdue (7)
22 Conceited — majestic (5)
23 Making an effort (6)
24 Population count (6)

DOWN

1 Fume (6)
2 Bed clothes (7)
3 Covering — a hen? (5)
5 Impervious to persuasion (7)
6 Fad (5)
7 Right away (informal) (6)
9 Those coming from Salzburg or Innsbruck, perhaps (9)
13 Radio show where listeners have their say (5-2)
14 Exuberant (7)
15 Phantom (6)
16 Rocks containing cavities lined with crystals (6)
18 Slightly drunk (5)
20 Plenty (5)

Solution see page 251

74

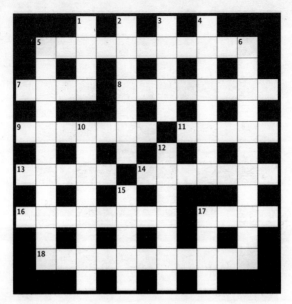

ACROSS

5 Same here! (4,3,4)
7 Unfriendly giant (4)
8 Meet (8)
9 Stranded (7)
11 Disjointed (5)
13 Police informer — baccy (5)
14 Member of a band of robbers (7)
16 Half-hearted (8)
17 Personal belongings (4)
18 Shrewd — a PhD twister (anag) (5-6)

DOWN

1 Dossier (4)
2 In a pile (7)
3 Seedless and flowerless green plants (5)
4 Short-lived (8)
5 Massive things that threaten to crush everything their way (11)
6 Run-of-the-mill (3-8)
10 Raised track across water or marshland (8)
12 Supposed source of technical glitches (7)
15 Florida resort on the Gulf of Mexico (5)
17 Intestines — backbone (4)

Solution see page 251

75

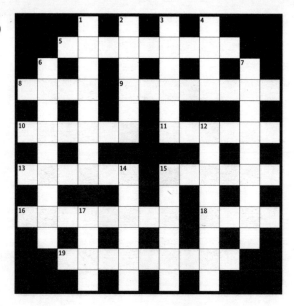

ACROSS

5 Member of the middle class? (9)

8 Manner (4)

9 Injury (which may need plastering?) (8)

10 Out of the way (6)

11 Small diving bird without webbed feet that feeds on river bed (6)

13 Cope with a difficult situation (4,2)

15 Charity race (3,3)

16 Only understandable by an enlightened inner circle (8)

18 Wander freely (4)

19 Someone easily put upon (4,5)

DOWN

1 Cloudburst (8)

2 Cold dessert (6)

3 Just deserts (6)

4 Hand, when clenched (4)

6 The other way round (4,5)

7 Against the rules (9)

12 Tiny puncture (8)

14 Equal status (6)

15 Element influencing a decision (6)

17 Sound a car horn (4)

Solution see page 251

76

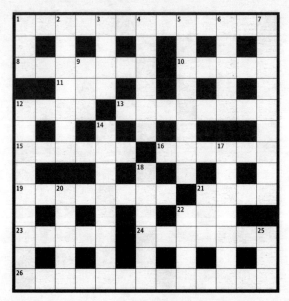

ACROSS

1 Ill in quarters (anag) — this should calm you (13)

8 Between the waist and chest (7)

10 Hoax (5)

11 It's used by anglers (and dowsers) (3)

12 Parcel of land (4)

13 Creative (8)

15 Platform (6)

16 Very keen (informal) (4-2)

19 The other day (8)

21 Curving (4)

22 Embargo (3)

23 Sports and live music venue (5)

24 Booty (7)

26 Repercussion (5-2,6)

DOWN

1 Hanks or Cruise? (3)

2 Automaton resembling a human (7)

3 £1 (informal) (4)

4 Tell (6)

5 Delicious (8)

6 Inadequate — brief (5)

7 Where monks tuck in (9)

9 Rubbish (3)

12 Book with a soft cover (9)

14 Go in the opposite direction (4,4)

17 VIP (7)

18 Shoe without fastening (4-2)

20 Set of beliefs (5)

21 Looking pale and tired (3)

22 Light brown — polish (4)

25 Furrow (3)

Solution see page 251

77

ACROSS

1 Immature (6)
4 Finish (3,2)
7 Debacle (6)
8 Extreme aversion (6)
9 Sandwich-maker (4)
10 Disregard (8)
12 Cosset (11)
17 Fairground attraction (3,5)
19 Bridge (4)
20 Inception (6)
21 Antagonism (6)
22 Loose (5)
23 Under the influence (of drink or drugs) (6)

DOWN

1 Professional outfit (7)
2 Calming (7)
3 First version of a new product (9)
4 Escort (5)
5 Force to take part (7)
6 Stunts (6)
11 Lent me oil (anag) — it's soothing (9)
13 Unfinished (7)
14 My Old Man's job (7)
15 Successfully demanded (7)
16 Take in (6)
18 Alarming — unshaven (5)

Solution see page 252

78

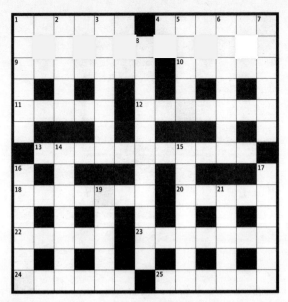

ACROSS

1 Haven (6)
4 Egyptian god of the underworld (6)
9 Nourish (7)
10 Celtic priest (5)
11 Minor actor in crowd scenes (5)
12 Disturbed (7)
13 ATM (4,7)
18 Rendering assistance (7)
20 Pass into disuse (5)
22 Most northerly of the Ionian Islands, called Kerkyra in Greek (5)
23 Precise (anag) — instructions for making something (7)
24 Truly (6)
25 Preserved for future use (6)

DOWN

1 A class of accommodation (6)
2 Before anything else (5)
3 Stew heavily seasoned with paprika (7)
5 __ Khan, Mayor of London (5)
6 Social gathering — Indian Ocean island (7)
7 Decorous (6)
8 Downtown British singer, b. 1932 (6,5)
14 Enticed (7)
15 Drunk (4-3)
16 Pretentiously stylish (6)
17 Tantalised (6)
19 Tall narrow wineglass (5)
21 Everyday product said to have been invented in China in about AD 100. (5)

Solution see page 252

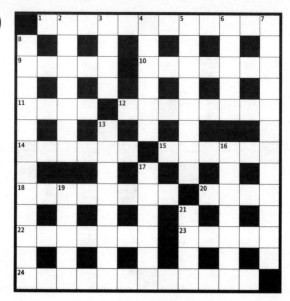

ACROSS

1 Problems in the early stages (7,5)
9 Beasts of burden (5)
10 Coffee shop coffee-maker (7)
11 Notice of someone's death (abbr) (4)
12 Illustrious (8)
14 American boss man (6)
15 Credence (6)
18 Forebear (8)
20 Adherent of an Indian religion (4)
22 To cut a long story short (2,5)
23 Like a imaginary line about which a body rotates (5)
24 Cold dessert made with puff pastry, cream etc (12)

DOWN

2 Roulette, salad, tea or thistle (7)
3 Stinging insect (4)
4 Collared (6)
5 Forgiven (8)
6 Norwegian playwright, who wrote all his plays in Danish, d. 1906 (5)
7 Rugby player (5-3,4)
8 Narrowness of outlook (12)
13 Castigate (8)
16 First (7)
17 confectionery made of caramelised sugar (6)
19 Group of plotters (5)
21 Surrealist painter, born in Catalonia, d. 1989 (4)

Solution see page 252

80

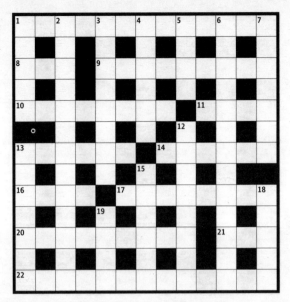

ACROSS

1 State of one's affairs (13)

8 Broad sash worn with a kimono (3)

9 Regarded with great respect (9)

10 Kind of goose or guitar (8)

11 Winkle-picker, for example (4)

13 Spring discharging hot water and steam (6)

14 South American pack animals (6)

16 Public houses (4)

17 Author of The Charge of the Light Brigade (8)

20 Study of language (9)

21 Venomous snake (3)

22 2002 James Bond movie (3,7,3)

DOWN

1 Material (5)

2 Loco (7,6)

3 Shown for the first time (8)

4 Ice cream with syrup or crushed fruit (6)

5 '__ and graces' — affectation of superiority (4)

6 Come up to scratch (3,3,7)

7 Sorrow (7)

12 Malawi's 'commercial and industrial capital' (8)

13 Grasped securely (7)

15 Lab vessel (6)

18 Fast — cold (5)

19 Word such as 'word' (4)

Solution see page 252

81

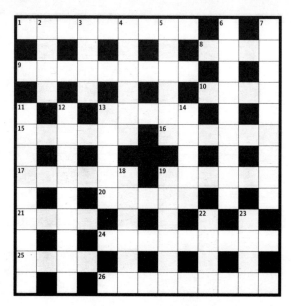

ACROSS

1 Expressing praise (9)
8 Expensive (4)
9 Lancashire seaside resort (9)
10 Stalk (4)
13 Stomach (5)
15 Spasmodic (6)
16 Merited (6)
17 Rebellion (6)
19 Deer's horn (6)
20 ___ Andronicus (Shakespearean tragedy) (5)
21 Rear — female deer (4)
24 Rise rapidly (9)
25 High ___ (1952 Western with Gary Cooper and Grace Kelly) (4)
26 Racing dog (9)

DOWN

2 Nautical hail (4)
3 Sea (literarily speaking) (4)
4 Go from place to place (6)
5 Fragments of stone, brick etc (6)
6 Four-sided figure (9)
7 Arabian camel (9)
11 Had no fear (anag) — in advance (9)
12 Treasure Island author (9)
13 Constructed (5)
14 Tales (5)
18 Itinerant who once mended pots and pans (6)
19 ___ Beardsley, exotic English book illustrator, d. 1898 aged 25 (6)
22 Mountain nymph spurned by Narcissus (4)
23 Observed (4)

Solution see page 253

82

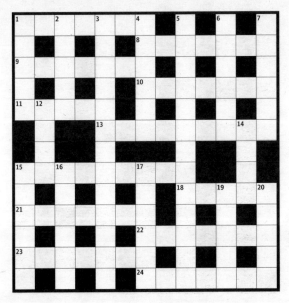

ACROSS

1 Snubs (7)
8 Accomplish (7)
9 Large crested pheasant — lop a few (anag) (7)
10 In the customary manner (2,5)
11 Exhausted (5)
13 Instant (9)
15 Butcher (9)
18 Chap (5)
21 Exclusive circle (7)
22 Learner (7)
23 Self-propelled underwater weapon (7)
24 In attendance (7)

DOWN

1 Know these to be experienced? (5)
2 It slows or stops progress (5)
3 One undecided as to which party to support (8,5)
4 Deep bow of salutation in Arabicspeaking countries (6)
5 Scapula (8,5)
6 She was transformed into a Gorgon by Athena and finally decapitated by Perseus (6)
7 I'll see (anag) — boy's name (6)
12 What Jack and Jill went up the hill with (4)
14 Conversation (4)
15 Devious (informal) (6)
16 Sign of important things to come (6)
17 A1 (3-3)
19 Light weight (5)
20 Upright (5)

Solution see page 253

83

ACROSS

1 Relapsing into bad ways (11)
9 Carefully listening (9)
10 Pasture (3)
11 Discourage (5)
13 Cream cakes (7)
14 Go too far (6)
15 Attest (6)
18 Pain in the middle or inner ear (7)
20 To do with an anatomical bulge or swelling (5)
21 Fasten (3)
22 Venetian merchant and explorer who wrote about Kublai Khan's China, d. 1324 (5,4)
24 Set up (11)

DOWN

2 Play section (3)
3 Similar in quality or character (7)
4 Linger — lurk (6)
5 Reside (5)
6 Invalidated (9)
7 With barely enough money for immediate needs (4,2,5)
8 Pink-flowered plant — confectionery item (11)
12 Young people (9)
16 Resembling mushrooms or toadstools? (7)
17 Cask (6)
19 Bass instrument of the viol family with about the range of a cello (abbr) (5)
23 Chart-topping number? (3)

Solution see page 253

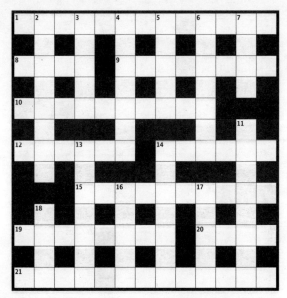

ACROSS

1 Housing (13)
8 Smash's partner in crime? (4)
9 Long dagger (8)
10 Excessively dramatic or emotional (10)
12 Cereal crop (6)
14 Proper (6)
15 Love letter (6-4)
19 Civic centre (4,4)
20 Manner (4)
21 Trout Quintet composer (5,8)

DOWN

2 Knitted jacket (8)
3 Circle round another object (5)
4 Bewilder (7)
5 Condescend (5)
6 Molasses (7)
7 In the process of finding out about (4)
11 Struggle to make any progress at all (8)
13 Middle East country (7)
14 Avoiding attention by moving carefully (7)
16 Plenty (informal) (5)
17 Release from military service (5)
18 3,600 seconds (4)

Solution see page 253

85

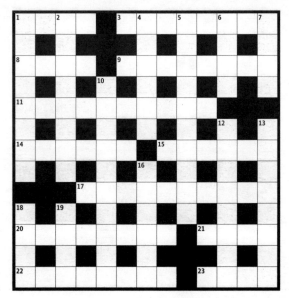

ACROSS

1 Put one's hands together (4)
3 Not friendly (8)
8 Heap (4)
9 Extremely strong (4-4)
11 Self-assurance (10)
14 Momentary pain (6)
15 Blood fluid (6)
17 Insurrection — one full turn (10)
20 Formal etiquette (8)
21 Lacking sensation (4)
22 Largest city in Westphalia, with a top flight football team (8)
23 Disappointing match result (4)

DOWN

1 Unoriginal people (8)
2 Legendary vanished island, swallowed by an earthquake (8)
4 Came close to (6)
5 Showing great attention to detail (10)
6 Record of scores in a round of golf (4)
7 Row — occupation (4)
10 Flexibility for interpretation — eg grim wool (anag) (6,4)
12 The Remains of the Day author (8)
13 Marijuana (8)
16 Name for Detroit and the music associated with it (6)
18 Went quickly (4)
19 Journey round a particular place or area (4)

Solution see page 254

86

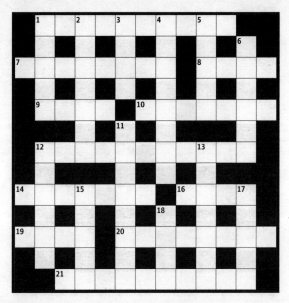

ACROSS

1 French fashion designer, d. 1971 (4,6)

7 Make abrupt changes of policy (4-4)

8 Small islands (4)

9 Small piece of paper for writing a note (4)

10 Painkiller (7)

12 Accelerate (6,5)

14 Servitude (7)

16 50% (4)

19 Kind of adventure (4)

20 Awful (8)

21 Asian country, independent since 1971 (10)

DOWN

1 Acute abdominal pain in babies and horses (5)

2 Mediterranean islander (7)

3 Male horse under the age of four (4)

4 Mountaineer who specialises in difficult climbs (8)

5 Spiral-horned antelope (5)

6 Repented (6)

11 Prickly creature (8)

12 Not limited in scope (6)

13 Scrutinise (7)

15 Kind of play (5)

17 Disgusting material (5)

18 Killer whale (4)

Solution see page 254

87

ACROSS

1 Study of handwriting (10)
7 Even — consistent (7)
8 Frozen dew (5)
10 Finished (4)
11 Easily deceived (8)
13 Biblical strong man (6)
15 Yet to be perused (6)
17 Sets right (8)
18 Loose scrum — rough up (4)
21 Greek letter equivalent to S (5)
22 Fetched (7)
23 Megaphone (10)

DOWN

1 Grumble — colic (5)
2 River at Stratford (4)
3 Minty sweet (6)
4 Means of rescue — crease on the palm (8)
5 Farewell (7)
6 Unwell (3,2,5)
9 Surveying instrument (10)
12 Area growing trees and shrubs (8)
14 Myopic cartoon character (2,5)
16 Country formerly part of Yugoslavia (6)
19 Make cross (5)
20 Hinged metal cover of an engine (4)

Solution see page 254

88

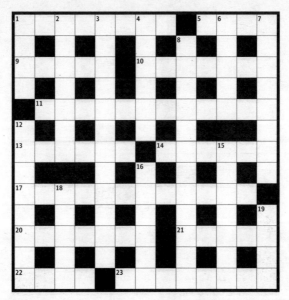

ACROSS

1 Computer programs (8)
5 Island where Napoleon was exiled in 1814 (4)
9 Intended (5)
10 Dizziness (7)
11 More and more (12)
13 In poor health (6)
14 Get in the way (6)
17 Stop just talking and get on with it! (3,3,6)
20 Country in the Horn of Africa (7)
21 Insinuate (5)
22 That being the case ... (2,2)
23 Uninformed (unlike this puzzle) (8)

DOWN

1 Japanese wrestling (4)
2 Facecloth (7)
3 Public house (8,4)
4 Divulge (6)
6 Prone or prostrate (5)
7 Faithful followers (8)
8 One-armed bandit (5,7)
12 Spring-flowering plants (8)
15 Regular oval shape (7)
16 Scribble (6)
18 Books of substance (5)
19 Votes in favour (4)

Solution see page 254

89

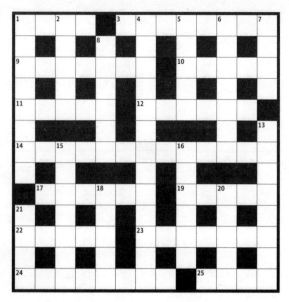

ACROSS

1 Ready, willing and able (4)

3 English county on the Bristol Channel (8)

9 Aridity (7)

10 Kick out (5)

11 Precious stone (5)

12 Regard with respect (6)

14 Not expected (13)

17 Predicament (6)

19 Plumbing problems (5)

22 Opposite of forte (5)

23 10,000 square meters (7)

24 Classification (8)

25 Great confusion (4)

DOWN

1 Restless seeker after amusement (8)

2 Civic head (5)

4 Black and white wading bird (13)

5 Vote for (5)

6 Panties (anag) — sagacious (7)

7 Thin flat slab used for roofing (4)

8 Fanatic (6)

13 Homer's mythical Greek hero of the Trojan War (8)

15 Pull in (7)

16 Royal residence (6)

18 Moving forward (5)

20 Proverb (5)

21 Long poem — awesome! (4)

Solution see page 255

90

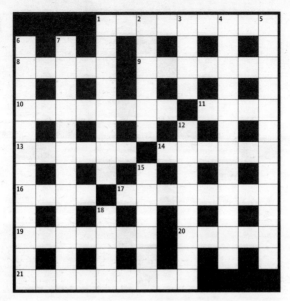

ACROSS

1 Find out (9)
8 Approaches (5)
9 Tommy or GI Joe? (7)
10 Unguent (8)
11 The Beehive State (4)
13 Small rounded stone (6)
14 Metal, Cu (6)
16 Seldom seen (4)
17 Co-operate (4,4)
19 Cosmetic applied to the cheeks (7)
20 Mariner's milieu (5)
21 Shown (9)

DOWN

1 Put together (8)
2 Croupier's workplace (6)
3 Purpose — function (4)
4 Greek comedy playwright, d. c.385 BC (12)
5 Part of the London Underground (8,4)
6 Matchless (12)
7 Lincolnshire town — 18th century painter (12)
12 Metonym for the Scottish Parliament (8)
15 Red wine from Bordeaux (6)
18 European freshwater fish (4)

Solution see page 255

91

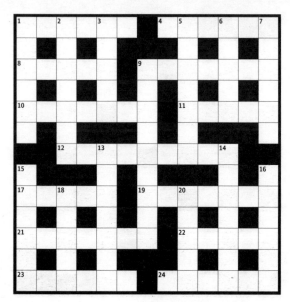

ACROSS

1 Sexual desire (6)
4 Absent-minded and disorganised (6)
8 Utter (5)
9 Pistol (7)
10 Begun (7)
11 Concur (5)
12 Criticise severely (9)
17 Abyss (5)
19 God of wine (7)
21 Sequoia (7)
22 Clearly expressed (5)
23 Indirect taxes on imports (6)
24 Fairground barker's exhortation (4,2)

DOWN

1 Very generous (6)
2 Abridge (anag) — military unit (7)
3 Lived (5)
5 Vocal composition, typically with choir and orchestra (7)
6 Striped predator (5)
7 Tugged sharply (6)
9 City in India and Pakistan (9)
13 Create music (7)
14 Principled (7)
15 Made afraid (6)
16 Exhausted (4,2)
18 Inspection of accounts (5)
20 Large stringed instrument (5)

Solution see page 255

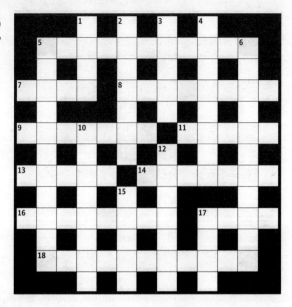

ACROSS

5 1964 Disney film with Julie Andrews (4,7)
7 Disastrous failure (4)
8 Plane(s) (8)
9 Fan (7)
11 Decease (5)
13 Earthy pigment, ranging in colour from light yellow to red (5)
14 Assuage (7)
16 London rail terminus (8)
17 Small opening in the skin (4)
18 Lacking distinctive features (11)

DOWN

1 Excursion (4)
2 Raiment (7)
3 Reject disdainfully (5)
4 Prime minister who made 16 Empress of India (8)
5 Curse (11)
6 Slogan advocating caution (6,5)
10 It's annoying (8)
12 Remainder (7)
15 Attempts (5)
17 Bodily suffering (4)

Solution see page 255

93

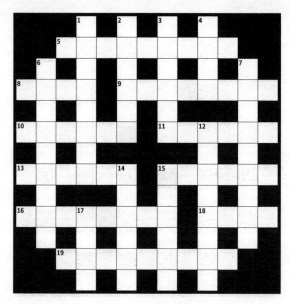

ACROSS

5 Chewing gum flavour (9)
8 Star Wars princess (4)
9 Period of chilly weather (4,4)
10 Eyesight (6)
11 Pertinacious (6)
13 Medical practitioner (6)
15 Purchased (6)
16 Greek sea god (8)
18 International cricket match (4)
19 Catalan capital (9)

DOWN

1 Beekeeper (8)
2 High-kicking dance (6)
3 Sauntered (6)
4 Concludes (4)
6 Punctuation mark (9)
7 Schematic (anag) — questions put to a candidate (9)
12 Greedy people (8)
14 Diminish (6)
15 Bracelet (6)
17 Dutch cheese (4)

Solution see page 256

94

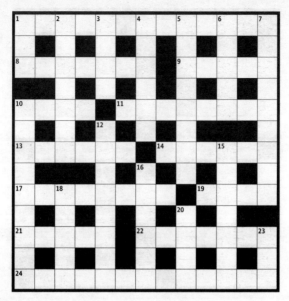

ACROSS

1 Hairdressing tool (used for for careful examination?) (4-5,4)
8 Got away (7)
9 Head of a male religious order (5)
10 Walk heavily (4)
11 Dashing, debonair young men (8)
13 Small quake (6)
14 Housing area (6)
17 Occasionally (3,3,2)
19 Rotate continuously (4)
21 Amundsen or Dahl? (5)
22 Excavate (7)
24 So (2,11)

DOWN

1 Enemy (3)
2 Well done! (4,3)
3 Gratuities (4)
4 Severe trial (6)
5 Despairing — pathetic (8)
6 Bulbous vegetable (5)
7 West Side Story composer (9)
10 Fragrant mixture (9)
12 Participated (6,2)
15 Common painkiller (7)
16 Cubic capacity — loudness (6)
18 Swiss currency unit (5)
20 Boyfriend (4)
23 Hasten (3)

Solution see page 256

95

ACROSS

1 Spirit distilled from wine (6)
4 Cut into small cubes (5)
7 They go with word (and also with copper, gold and silver) (6)
8 Gilt or bronzed metallic ware (6)
9 Catholic church service (4)
10 Not easily satisfied (8)
12 Feeling of dread (11)
17 Just — proper (8)
19 Uncontaminated (4)
20 Mute (6)
21 Drinker (in a pub?) (6)
22 Freshwater fish of the carp family (5)
23 Crunchy salad vegetable (6)

DOWN

1 Pompously inflated language (7)
2 Professional dancer or singer (7)
3 Incredulity (9)
4 Classical Greek building style (5)
5 Hot Spanish sausage (7)
6 One obliged to do menial work (6)
11 Ready for employment (9)
13 Paraphernalia of high office (7)
14 Beseech (7)
15 Children's room (7)
16 It can rub things out (6)
18 Ordinal number (5)

Solution see page 256

96

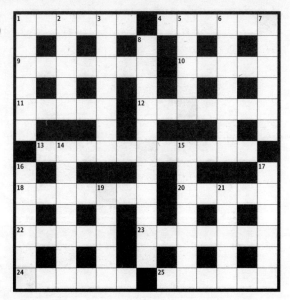

ACROSS

1 Nautical kitchen (6)
4 Blanket-like cloak that goes over the head (6)
9 Female singer (7)
10 Peaceful scene (5)
11 Distribute (5)
12 Expression of approval (5,2)
13 Expressing affection (6-5)
18 Small country house? (7)
20 Cheerful (5)
22 Scent (5)
23 Harsh (7)
24 Be incensed (6)
25 Nostril partition (6)

DOWN

1 Envelope that lifts a flying balloon (6)
2 Continuation of a coat collar (5)
3 Flexible (7)
5 Not settled (5)
6 Quartz, say (7)
7 Rectangle with unequal adjacent sides (6)
8 Upper-class twit (6,5)
14 Consequence (7)
15 Support (a cause) (7)
16 On the other side of (6)
17 Plaster of Paris, say (6)
19 I'm tearing my hair out! (5)
21 Perch (5)

Solution see page 256

97

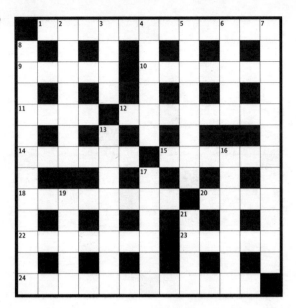

ACROSS

1 From KwaZulu-Natal? (5,7)
9 Levitate (5)
10 Troglodyte (7)
11 Vivacity (4)
12 Thin condiment made with fermented beans (3,5)
14 The Beaver State (6)
15 Main Japanese island (6)
18 Machine for cutting grass (8)
20 Small inland island (4)
22 Ardent early supporter (7)
23 Professorship (5)
24 First English sea captain to circumnavigate the globe (7,5)

DOWN

2 Preclude (7)
3 Limited period of time (4)
4 Fix firmly (6)
5 Emendation (8)
6 Welsh Wales (5)
7 Assertions that do not follow from the evidence (3,9)
8 Principal adviser to the person in charge of a large organisation (5,2,5)
13 Skin-deep (8)
16 Indulge in horseplay (7)
17 Parliamentary break (6)
19 Red (and white) wine from a region of northern Spain (5)
21 Wound mark (4)

Solution see page 257

98

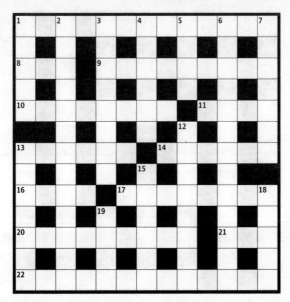

ACROSS

1 How to spin a car quickly (9,4)
8 Palindromic passerine bird (3)
9 Anecdotist (9)
10 Couch potato (8)
11 Place with a tower that leans (4)
13 Chipper (6)
14 Lose this and you're out of the competition (3,3)
16 (Make a) mistake (informal) (4)
17 Wake-up call bird (8)
20 Fundamental principle (9)
21 Do it now! (3)
22 I'm so relieved! (5,8)

DOWN

1 Accommodation for those away from home (5)
2 Something in which I wouldn't be interested (3,2,3,2,3)
3 Garden washing facility (8)
4 Grow by addition (6)
5 Europe's most active volcano (4)
6 Program that displays how to interact with a computer (4,9)
7 Provide the commentary for a film, for example (7)
12 Wall in a ship (8)
13 Run slowly (7)
15 Albert II's principality (6)
18 Large water lily (5)
19 It's for reading (4)

Solution see page 257

99

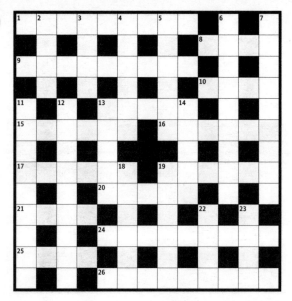

ACROSS

1 Study of the origin and nature of the universe (9)

8 Travel pass (4)

9 Deepen (9)

10 Mock (4)

13 Pale purple colour (5)

15 Recluse (6)

16 Polish capital (6)

17 Row (6)

19 Informal eatery serving wine (6)

20 Steel tower supporting power lines (5)

21 Bouquet (4)

24 Established by written law (9)

25 Money paid to the unemployed (4)

26 Part of a limb farthest from the torso (9)

DOWN

2 Porker's noise (4)

3 Submissive (4)

4 Suddenly snap (4,2)

5 Hoot of laughter (6)

6 Variety (9)

7 Vendor with handcart (6,3)

11 Feet treatment (9)

12 Sharp — bang on (9)

13 Became animated (3,2)

14 Where on an aircraft passengers are carried (5)

18 (Study of) sentence structure (6)

19 Straw hat (6)

22 Article (4)

23 (Of sparkling wine) very dry (4)

Solution see page 257

100

ACROSS

1 Skeleton of older motor vehicles (7)

8 Beat easily — recount (anag) (7)

9 Expected to be warm and dry (3,4)

10 Demanding considerable mental effort and skill (7)

11 California-based multinational IT company (5)

13 Container for cold cubes (3,6)

15 Poetry without regular rhythm (4,5)

18 Part of the body gazed at by those engaged in complacent selfabsorption (5)

21 Black bird 'of Rheims' which was canonised as Saint Jem Crow (7)

22 List (7)

23 South American monkey (7)

24 Underground pipe carrying flammable substance (3,4)

DOWN

1 Spanish seaside (5)

2 Misbehave (3,2)

3 1978 'shoot 'em up' arcade game developed by Tomohiro Nishikado (5,8)

4 Attack ground targets from a lowflying plane (6)

5 Elizabeth I (4,5,4)

6 Open a bottle of wine (6)

7 One-room accommodation (6)

12 Henry VIII's sixth wife (4)

14 Tranquil rest (4)

15 Tex-Mex dish of grilled meat served as a taco on a tortilla (6)

16 Lodge (6)

17 Having a dispute (6)

19 Here it is! (5)

20 Stay in bed in the morning (3-2)

Solution see page 257

101

ACROSS

1 Noticeable (11)
9 Strip on a guitar — ref Bardot (anag) (9)
10 Tiny (3)
11 Cause to move forward (5)
13 Sling your hook! (4,3)
14 Join the army? (6)
15 Cask for liquids, butter, salt or fish (6)
18 Operation to shift people and supplies with planes or helicopters (7)
20 Grade of a Bachelor's degree (5)
21 Pedal digit (3)
22 Powerful tractor with a blade in front (9)
24 Biblical figure who returns, having repented of former extravagant behaviour (8,3)

DOWN

2 Wrath (3)
3 Morsels of party food (7)
4 Out of condition (6)
5 South–west Spanish port (5)
6 Big Apple native (3,6)
7 Work's do (6,5)
8 Not thorough (11)
12 Arctic animal (5,4)
16 One who does not recognise your god (7)
17 German POW camp (6)
19 Between the sheets (2,3)
23 Where wild animals are housed (3)

Solution see page 258

102

ACROSS

1 Performing less well these days (4,4,5)
8 Hoodoo (4)
9 Screen (8)
10 Touch-and-go (10)
12 Traditional Alpine peasant costume (6)
14 Diversion (6)
15 Tropical Asian plant grown for its pungent root — rig segment (anag) (4,6)
19 Febrile (8)
20 Three of a kind (4)
21 It's hard to say (6-7)

DOWN

2 Polluted shower (4,4)
3 Poisonous (5)
4 Not artificial (7)
5 Simultaneous discharge of guns (5)
6 Go to again (7)
7 Cloud of water droplets (4)
11 24 December to 6 January? (8)
13 Rainy day money? (4,3)
14 Crufts, for example (3,4)
16 Select group (5)
17 Buttocks (5)
18 Toy bricks (4)

Solution see page 258

103

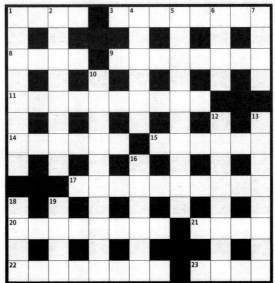

ACROSS

1 Indonesian island, home to over half the country's population (4)

3 General (8)

8 Tropical shrub, source of drug (4)

9 (Of a hairstyle) puffed out (8)

11 Financial ruin (10)

14 Canada's capital (6)

15 Basque game played with basket rackets (6)

17 Decadence (10)

20 Negatively charged subatomic particle (8)

21 Tibetan monk (4)

22 Further comment at the bottom of the page (8)

23 Happy (4)

DOWN

1 Authoritarian footwear? (8)

2 Locality (8)

4 I've spilt it! (6)

5 Skilfulness in avoiding wasted time and effort (10)

6 One of a line of tablet computers (4)

7 Courage (informal) (4)

10 Bullied (10)

12 Fit together tightly — violated (anag) (8)

13 Old Line State (8)

16 Jumbo rider (6)

18 Page in a book (4)

19 Right of rejection (4)

Solution see page 258

104

ACROSS

1 American crime syndicate, having close relations with the Sicilian Mafia (4,6)

7 Grandfather, say (or a grandfather clock?) (3-5)

8 Nibble (4)

9 Electrical sound (4)

10 First artificial Earth satellite, orbiting from October 1957 to January 1958 (7)

12 Chimney climber and repairer (11)

14 Small acting role (3,4)

16 Crossword arrangement (4)

19 Complain(t) (4)

20 Australian state formerly known as Van Diemen's Land (8)

21 Antics (10)

DOWN

1 Star (abbr) (5)

2 That will teach you! (2,5)

3 Denomination (4)

4 Shell fragments (8)

5 Prove to be false (5)

6 Endangered (2,4)

11 Drink before a meal (8)

12 Name of Ho Chi Minh City until 1976 (6)

13 Medium for radio and television broadcasting (7)

15 Puss In Boots, for example (abbr) (5)

17 Supernatural being, the object of worship (5)

18 Scandinavian capital, called Christiania until 1925 (4)

Solution see page 258

105

ACROSS

1 When Jesus' entry into Jerusalem is celebrated by Christians (4,6)

7 Claptrap (7)

8 French philosopher associated with 'absurdism', friend of Jean-Paul Sartre, d. 1960 (5)

10 French comic actor and film-maker, d. 1982 (4)

11 Plant producing drooping white flowers in late winter (8)

13 Small purple plum-like fruit (6)

15 Austro-Bohemian Romantic composer and conductor, d. 1911 (6)

17 Bitterness (8)

18 Port on the Caspian Sea, capital of Azerbaijan (4)

21 Moral story (5)

22 Springtime post that's danced around (7)

23 City in North Rhine–Westphalia, birthplace of Anne of Cleves (10)

DOWN

1 Live in squalor (informal) (3,2)

2 Soft heavy metal (4)

3 Large stone statue with a lion's body and a human head (6)

4 Ties, for example (8)

5 Senior naval officer (7)

6 Small dense star (5,5)

9 Fab! (5-5)

12 Amorphous (8)

14 Large African black-and-white stork — rub a moa (anag) (7)

16 Paint that dries to a hard glossy finish (6)

19 First name of the politician appointed German chancellor in January 1933 (5)

20 Text error (4)

Solution see page 259

106

ACROSS

1 Look after yourself! (4,4)

5 University academic (abbr) (4)

9 Book of blank pages organising photographs, stamp collections etc (5)

10 Old brass instrument with a clear tone (used in calls for action?) (7)

11 Stubbornly resistant (12)

13 Long-bodied reptile (given to lounging?) (6)

14 Cocktail of white rum and lime juice (6)

17 Small electrical appliance for the kitchen (3-2,7)

20 Very old (7)

21 Tangle — disentangle (5)

22 Chopped meat mixed with potatoes and then browned (4)

23 Peril (8)

DOWN

1 Salver (4)

2 City at the confluence of the Rhine and Moselle (7)

3 Fail badly (informal) (4,1,7)

4 Ornate — extravagant (6)

6 Indian yoghurt side dish (5)

7 Practical purpose (8)

8 Narrative sequence of humorous sketches (7,5)

12 Done quickly and without thought (8)

15 Become frozen (3,4)

16 Chin beard, trimmed to a point (6)

18 An ancient people that once inhabited parts of Scotland (5)

19 Put to the sword (4)

Solution see page 259

107

ACROSS

1 One much concerned with his appearance (informal) (4)

3 Miniature hourglass, used in the kitchen (3,5)

9 Small medicated sweet (7)

10 Nettled (5)

11 Bowler's approach (3-2)

12 Middle Eastern country invaded by Iraq in 1990, leading to the Gulf War (6)

14 Bank notes with no real existence or worth (8,5)

17 Sharp pain in the side (6)

19 Relating to the centre (5)

22 Pull suddenly (5)

23 Kingdom lying between France and the Netherlands (7)

24 Number each leaf in a publication (8)

25 Bring off mother's milk (4)

DOWN

1 State of stagnation (8)

2 12 (5)

4 Alpha to omega (5,8)

5 Pitch (5)

6 One, plus six noughts (7)

7 Uncivil (4)

8 Buy cheaply (4,2)

13 Plant of the primrose family with upswept petals and patterned leaves (8)

15 Zero (7)

16 Deaden (6)

18 Symbol (5)

20 Legal offence (5)

21 Vessel (4)

Solution see page 259

108

ACROSS

1 Conical pastry with whipped filling (5,4)

8 Island member of the European Union (5)

9 Absorbent paper used to dry writing in ink (7)

10 Looker (without microscope or telescope?) (5,3)

11 Captain of the submarine Nautilus (4)

13 Instead (2,4)

14 Improve (6)

16 In addition (4)

17 Non-combatant (8)

19 Stinking (7)

20 Came about (5)

21 With panache (9)

DOWN

1 Ship or boat equipment dealer (8)

2 Human organism formed during the early stages of pregnancy (6)

3 State of mind (4)

4 Expected soon (2,3,7)

5 Shockable (6-6)

6 They free others from bondage (12)

7 Improbable (1,6,5)

12 Chastity (8)

15 Excessively sentimental art; considered to be in bad taste (6)

18 Indian prime minister (4)

109

ACROSS

1 My word! (2,4)
4 Aromatic ointment (6)
8 One getting out of bed (5)
9 Wool fabric with a colourful swirled pattern (7)
10 Pigeon lover? (7)
11 Vast multitude (5)
12 1969 American music festival (9)
17 Postponed (2,3)
19 (Ridicule with) mockery (7)
21 Delight (7)
22 Godhead (5)
23 Dark sweet ale (6)
24 In short supply (6)

DOWN

1 Deprived (of) (6)
2 Moments ago (4,3)
3 La Traviata composer (5)
5 Sound of a sneeze (7)
6 From the sun (5)
7 Violent disturbance (6)
9 Semi-soft cows' milk cheese from the Loire, developed by Trappist monks in the 19th century (4,5)
13 Made a pig of oneself (7)
14 Device for rapping (7)
15 Cram to learn relevant facts (4,2)
16 Main course (6)
18 Experience (5)
20 Copy for satirical effect (5)

Solution see page 260

110

ACROSS

5 Dessert eaten all over the world — ringed Cupid (anag) (4,7)

7 Causing a dull and steady pain (4)

8 Formality in bearing and appearance (8)

9 Nemanja Matic, Aleksander Kolarov or Nemanja Vidic, for example (7)

11 Refreshing and herbal (5)

13 Very angry (informal) (5)

14 Look after someone else's children for a period (7)

16 Brawny sexy guy? (8)

17 Unique — fish (4)

18 Overwhelmed by work (in the winter?) (6,5)

DOWN

1 Distastefully sentimental (informal) (4)

2 Quip (7)

3 Model of perfection (5)

4 Manliness (8)

5 Device for keeping strings taut (6,5)

6 Someone like the hero in Jack and the Beanstalk? (5–6)

10 Shoeless (8)

12 Pernicious (7)

15 What Adam drank? (5)

17 15 with bubbles (4)

Solution see page 260

111

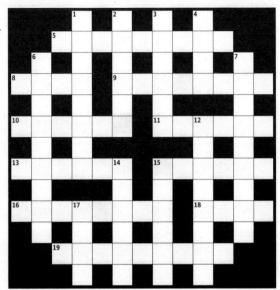

ACROSS

5 Boisterous comedy involving collisions and practical jokes (9)

8 Clarified butter used in Indian cookery (4)

9 Unrealistic (8)

10 Ask (6)

11 With great force (6)

13 Hard mineral consisting of silicon dioxide in crystal form (6)

15 Canny (6)

16 Give heart to (8)

18 Obnoxious lot (slang) (4)

19 Burrowing mammal covered with strong horny plates (9)

DOWN

1 Underlying (8)

2 Cloudy — obscure (6)

3 Chamber (6)

4 Reverberation (4)

6 Whatsit — my thin mug (anag) (9)

7 Small northern grey gull with a shrill cry sounding like its name (9)

12 Grotesque waterspout (8)

14 Narrow belt in the heavens divided into 12 signs for astrological purposes (6)

15 Illuminated by a star during the day (6)

17 Bhindi (4)

Solution see page 260

112

ACROSS

1 Wild horse, not yet broken in (7,6)

8 Sent a message via the airwaves (7)

9 Smooth line containing no straight portions or no sharp angles (5)

10 Scourge (4)

11 Intentionally unobtrusive (8)

13 Astonished (6)

14 Mover on ice (6)

17 Catholic prayer (4,4)

19 Pack away (4)

21 (Of an angle) less than 90° (5)

22 Miscellany (7)

24 Texas (4,4,5)

DOWN

1 Music unit (3)

2 Solo passage towards the end of a piece of music (7)

3 Golf club (4)

4 Large wading bird, like a curlew — two dig (anag) (6)

5 Small bun (said to look solid!) (4,4)

6 Cheek (informal) (5)

7 Topple (9)

10 Inflatable object for play by the sea (5,4)

12 With no apparent gaps between one part and the next (8)

15 Fairy queen (7)

16 Black Sea peninsula (6)

18 Put ashes into an appropriate container (5)

20 Positive thing (4)

23 The First Lady (3)

Solution see page 260

113

ACROSS

1 The Silver State (6)
4 Winner (abbr) (5)
7 Not written in a key (6)
8 Mysteries (6)
9 Star suddenly expanding (4)
10 Metal, Ti (8)
12 Fool (informal) — necked a hulk (anag) (11)
17 Something precipitating an event (8)
19 Provoke (4)
20 East (6)
21 Go (6)
22 Compare (5)
23 Good-looking (6)

DOWN

1 Web (7)
2 South Pacific country, where Prince Philip was revered as a spiritual figure (7)
3 Item pressed to remove computer text etc (6,3)
4 Around (5)
5 Type of coffee bean (7)
6 Sacred songs in praise to God (6)
11 Number of players on the pitch at the start of a football match (6–3)
13 Cavil (7)
14 Incise (7)
15 Clerical office — yearned (anag) (7)
16 Shoal (6)
18 Cloth made with flax fibres (5)

Solution see page 261

114

ACROSS

1 Shove (6)
4 Go after (6)
9 Burnt sugar used to flavour puddings (7)
10 Not illuminated (5)
11 Supplementary (5)
12 Happy — substance (7)
13 Hapless (11)
18 Reject (7)
20 Dark brown (5)
22 Fit for a queen (or king) (5)
23 Destructive (7)
24 Armless couch (6)
25 Inferior (6)

DOWN

1 Item of outerwear (6)
2 Swagger (5)
3 Pain — a bum log (anag) (7)
5 Reversal of a previous decision (1-4)
6 Not in the red (7)
7 Extensive country landed property (6)
8 Tall structures that tell the time (5,6)
14 Old-fashioned posy (7)
15 Feed (7)
16 Cherished (6)
17 Fastidious — easily offended (6)
19 Treasure (5)
21 Ponder — issue (5)

Solution see page 261

115

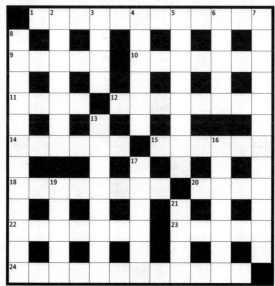

ACROSS

1 Poorly thought out (3-9)
9 Wear down (5)
10 Rod used in making thread (7)
11 Fake (4)
12 Distinguished (8)
14 Buy back (6)
15 Breed (6)
18 Dodge (8)
20 Even-handed (4)
22 Exploitation to the point of diminishing returns (7)
23 Problems — difficulties (informal) (5)
24 Baa, Baa, Black Sheep and Mary, Mary, Quite Contrary, say (7,5)

DOWN

2 Do alter (anag) — a sporty one-piece (7)
3 Hints (4)
4 Cosy up (6)
5 Move abroad (8)
6 Technology for recording moving images (5)
7 Where an actor prepares (8,4)
8 Sponsored set (anag) — it's used to eat pudding (12)
13 Hearten (8)
16 Mixture (7)
17 Cure (6)
19 Grim (5)
21 Skin eruption (4)

Solution see page 261

116

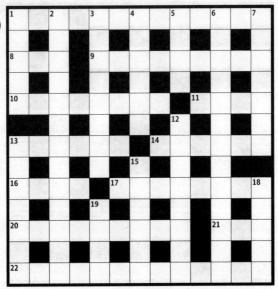

ACROSS

1 Befits grunter (anag) — not a safe pair of hands? (13)

8 Health resort with a spring (3)

9 Handlebar or pencil? (9)

10 Expels (5,3)

11 Deteriorate through corrosion (4)

13 Kettle, say? (6)

14 Skewer (6)

16 Change direction (4)

17 Oblique (8)

20 Controversial issue (3,6)

21 Stray (3)

22 Open-air drama (6,7)

DOWN

1 Reduced to the essentials (5)

2 One moving from one region to another to settle — trims tarragon (anag) (13)

3 Caught in a net and unable to escape (8)

4 Embarrassing blunder (4-2)

5 Record — piece of music (4)

6 Fillip (13)

7 Darling (informal) (7)

12 Not a fussy eater? (8)

13 Collections of things to be handled together (7)

15 Toddler (6)

18 Short and to the point (5)

19 Traditional knowledge (4)

Solution see page 261

117

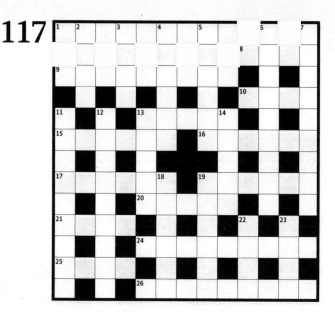

ACROSS

1 A game of one? (9)
8 Tiny creature (4)
9 Van Gogh's Chair, for example (5,4)
10 Singer Lynn — fashion designer Wang (4)
13 Billie Holiday's 1939 protest song about lynching, Strange ___ (5)
15 Harvesting tool with a curved blade (6)
16 Roman goddess of the dawn (6)
17 Pilot (6)
19 Writing or drawing instrument (6)
20 Instructor (5)
21 Coy (4)
24 Punch-up (4,5)
25 Rowing boat's propellers (4)
26 Unwise (9)

DOWN

2 Swear word (4)
3 To no purpose (4)
4 Fascination (6)
5 Palm leaf fibre (6)
6 Vital power (4,5)
7 Open to discussion (9)
11 It takes you up and down a building — or a castle (anag) (9)
12 Player's tally (9)
13 Buoyant object (5)
14 Potato or yam? (5)
18 Belief that it's best to bare all! (6)
19 Bill (6)
22 Soft — not bitter (4)
23 Keep it up when life's tough (4)

Solution see page 262

118

ACROSS

1 Run for it (7)
8 As a group (2,5)
9 Momentum (7)
10 Bent (7)
11 Criminal (5)
13 As a result (9)
15 Real — hue intact (anag) (9)
18 Give way (5)
21 Corresponds (7)
22 Woven material (7)
23 Middle-of-the-road safety device (7)
24 Turned round (7)

DOWN

1 Inflexible — demanding (5)
2 Greatly dismay (5)
3 It's used for shiny shoes, belts and bags (6,7)
4 Deliver from danger (6)
5 Escape from danger (9,4)
6 Phony (6)
7 Weed (a source of irritation) (6)
12 Beige (4)
14 Support — mode of transport (4)
15 Organisation (6)
16 Convict considered safe and granted special privileges (6)
17 Sample (6)
19 Kick out (5)
20 Serious apprehension (5)

Solution see page 262

119

ACROSS

1 Cartoon adversaries since 1940 (3,3,5)
9 Unwell — rude (3-6)
10 Drain (3)
11 Mustardseed or Peaseblossom, say (5)
13 Liberate (3,4)
14 Sign (6)
15 Textile made from unbleached cotton (6)
18 Turned in (7)
20 Machine tool used on wood or metal (5)
21 Parrot — gorilla (3)
22 Disparage — IT grandee (anag) (9)
24 Not anticipated (8,3)

DOWN

2 Dolt (3)
3 Disciple (7)
4 Ready to drop off (6)
5 Kind of heron (5)
6 Self-discipline (9)
7 Refreshing pause (6,5)
8 Pro esteemed (anag) — dashboard gauge (11)
12 Neither here nor there (2-7)
16 Claimed (7)
17 Polish city, birthplace of Solidarity (6)
19 Broadcast medium (5)
23 Fuss (3)

Solution see page 262

ACROSS

1 Ever irritable (anag) — beyond recovery (13)

8 Simple — French mother (4)

9 Creamy yellow flowering spring plant (8)

10 Red Riding Hood's rescuer (10)

12 Caucasian Chalk ___ , 1948 Brecht play (6)

14 Sports adjudicator (6)

15 St Jude is their patron saint (4,6)

19 Earmark (8)

20 Sign of sorrow (4)

21 Without real enthusiasm (4-9)

DOWN

2 Language used effectively to please or persuade (8)

3 Edit (5)

4 Extreme joy (7)

5 Occur (5)

6 Delivery from above? (7)

7 Shed (4)

11 Rapid decline (4,4)

13 Cancel (4,3)

14 Hazy (7)

16 Post — bet (5)

17 Release (5)

18 Pro-independence Scottish political party founded in March (4)

Solution see page 262

121

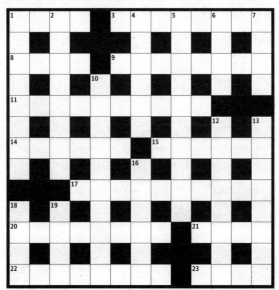

ACROSS

1 Golly! (4)
3 Alpha female? (5,3)
8 Orderly (4)
9 Dissembling (8)
11 Absurd (10)
14 Render powerless (6)
15 Male lover financially supported by a woman (6)
17 Theatrical stand-in (10)
20 Critic (8)
21 Healthy — source of water (4)
22 Comfortably off (4-2-2)
23 Cook slowly in liquid (4)

DOWN

1 Localised decomposition of body tissue (8)
2 Soft silvery metal, Sc (8)
4 Rowdy (6)
5 Devotee — Seth is a nut (anag) (10)
6 Attachment (4)
7 East of ___ , 1952 Steinbeck novel (4)
10 Film audition (6,4)
12 Cenotaph or shrine (8)
13 Significant setback (4,4)
16 Celebrity — story (6)
18 Sprouted (4)
19 Rounded like an egg (4)

Solution see page 263

122

ACROSS

1 Close calls (4,6)
7 Treasured hand-me-down (8)
8 Go under (4)
9 Team (4)
10 He's made to carry the can (4,3)
12 Unrealistic aspiration (3,2,3,3)
14 Explanatory drawing (7)
16 Sound pleased with oneself (4)
19 Complaint (of cattle?) (4)
20 Magnificence (8)
21 Wet and unkempt (10)

DOWN

1 Essential requirements (5)
2 Cut, while retaining the essential elements (7)
3 Daydream (4)
4 Understanding of the feelings of others (8)
5 Artist's stand (5)
6 To an excessive degree (6)
11 Piece of darkroom equipment (8)
12 Briefed beforehand (6)
13 Layered sweet pastry, often filled with apple (7)
15 Embarrassing slip-up (5)
17 Coiled (5)
18 Sharp flavour (4)

Solution see page 263

123

ACROSS

1 Where to sit at a live performance (10)

7 Foodie (7)

8 Finish the last of the job (3,2)

10 Main tower within the walls of a medieval castle (4)

11 The very top (8)

13 Focused (6)

15 Foul rising vapours (6)

17 Setting (8)

18 Too cute (4)

21 Pilotless aircraft (5)

22 (Take) refuge (7)

23 Presumption (10)

DOWN

1 (Theatrically) a remark just for the audience (5)

2 Cylindrical metal container (4)

3 Argument — proposal (6)

4 Starry-eyed (8)

5 Empties luggage (7)

6 Spineless (4-6)

9 Repeat ride (anag) — a place to stay in town (4-1-5)

12 Clothing from Fair Isle, say (8)

14 Mark on a list as completed (4,3)

16 Contaminate (6)

19 Funny and clever (5)

20 Village fundraising event (4)

Solution see page 263

124

ACROSS

1 Anxious uncertainty (8)
5 Fit of shivering and shaking (4)
9 Embarrassing outburst (5)
10 Earth, air, fire or water? (7)
11 Obstacle race — late speeches (anag) (12)
13 Fixed (6)
14 Influence (6)
17 Able to keep out wind and rain (12)
20 Enter uninvited (7)
21 Conscious (5)
22 Gain — win (4)
23 Car feature designed to prevent whiplash injuries (8)

DOWN

1 Strip of material worn around the waist or over the shoulder (4)
2 Stayed in bed later than normal (5,2)
3 The very last moment (8,4)
4 Humming (6)
6 Garbo or Thunberg? (5)
7 Urgent appeal (8)
8 In future (12)
12 Pale colour (3-5)
15 Touchy — controversial (7)
16 Stop right there! (6)
18 Cast member (5)
19 They can be cold or itchy! (4)

Solution see page 263

125

ACROSS

1 A very long time (4)
3 Unjust (8)
9 Upstart (7)
10 Thorny evergreen shrub with bright yellow flowers (5)
11 Additional — spare (5)
12 Assign to a specific task (6)
14 Get to the point (3,2,3,5)
17 Plan of action (6)
19 Employment (5)
22 Unusual and rather shocking (5)
23 Process of gradual assimilation (7)
24 Old toll gate — true pink (anag) (8)
25 Small earring held in a body piercing (4)

DOWN

1 Come near (8)
2 Third rock from the sun? (5)
4 Chuckled to Ron (anag) — 24/7 (5,3,5)
5 The _ _ _ Watch, Rembrandt's painting of a militia company (5)
6 Hard plastic laminate used for worktops (7)
7 Alcoholic residue (4)
8 Odd character (6)
13 No longer with us (8)
15 Betrayer (7)
16 Intimate (informal) (6)
18 Make fast (3,2)
20 Plus (5)
21 It could be vintage (or free!) (4)

Solution see page 264

126

ACROSS

1 Wooing (9)
8 Escape (5)
9 Financial institution that underwrites risks (7)
10 Utterly exhausted (3-5)
11 Edible tuber (informal) (4)
13 Just about (6)
14 Structure equipped to drill for petroleum or gas (3,3)
16 Cargo (4)
17 Extravagant promotion or fuss (8)
19 Rules of language (7)
20 Pyromaniac's criminal activity (5)
21 Rota (9)

DOWN

1 Convincing (8)
2 As one (6)
3 Heads or tails? (4)
4 Way of buying something on the never-never (4,8)
5 Where troops get their marching orders? (6,6)
6 One who inspires others — halting glide (anag) (7,5)
7 Noisy crime prevention device (7,5)
12 Stream powering a waterwheel (4,4)
15 Croatian capital (6)
18 Take out (4)

Solution see page 264

127

ACROSS

1 Suit (6)
4 Spoil (6)
8 Greek water nymph (5)
9 Lacking in assertiveness (7)
10 Suppress — bird (7)
11 Edition (5)
12 Far-seeing (5-4)
17 The Jolly Swagman's dance? (5)
19 Key person in an activity (7)
21 Build-up of items needing attention (7)
22 Significant influence (5)
23 Person who counts votes (6)
24 Separate (6)

DOWN

1 Dismiss (6)
2 Atmosphere (7)
3 Template (5)
5 Fox (7)
6 Assumed name (5)
7 Stank (6)
9 Pork wedge (anag) — it could easily go off (6,3)
13 Small, fast-running species of antelope (7)
14 Proof of qualification (7)
15 Worthless (3-3)
16 Grass (6)
18 Pub — neighbour (5)
20 Mother-of-pearl (5)

Solution see page 264

128

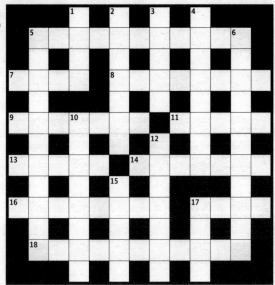

ACROSS

5 Meal eaten at work (6,5)
7 Stuck-up individual (4)
8 Storage item (8)
9 Drug — trance (7)
11 Disreputable (5)
13 Thickset (5)
14 Covered entrance with columns (7)
16 Spiny sea creature with five or more arms (8)
17 Tattered (4)
18 Patriotic fervour — into animals (anag) (11)

DOWN

1 Strike-breaker (4)
2 It keeps pot hot (3,4)
3 Horrid semi-liquid food (5)
4 Disrespectful (8)
5 Press it in a crisis (5,6)
6 Reckless (person) (5-6)
10 Bear (8)
12 Proceed (2,5)
15 Person not yet an adult (5)
17 Graft — grind (4)

Solution see page 264

129

ACROSS

5 Coolness under pressure (9)

8 Block of ice (4)

9 Fixed (8)

10 Colourless gas used as fuel, C2H6 (6)

11 In a way (4,2)

13 Tobacco user (6)

15 Ingratiating (6)

16 In an earliest stage — evil ramp (anag) (8)

18 Rational (4)

19 Black tie or smart casual, for example (5,4)

DOWN

1 Skin treatment (4,4)

2 Burst into flames (6)

3 Bits of uneaten cake — I'm surprised! (6)

4 Tree branch (4)

6 Regulars — consumers (9)

7 Share set aside (9)

12 ___ in Blue, 1924 George Gershwin composition (8)

14 Prepare for an exam (6)

15 Join the ends together (6)

17 Gloom (4)

Solution see page 265

130

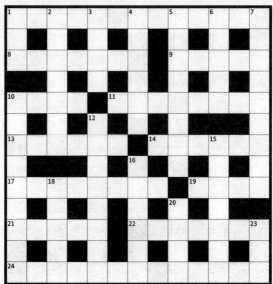

ACROSS

1 Skewer for party food (8,5)
8 Fruit-growing area (7)
9 Silent and out of sight (5)
10 ___ Dunn, author of Up the Junction (1963) (4)
11 Fragile exterior (not to be walked on!) (8)
13 Follow secretly (6)
14 Pointless — ineffective (2,4)
17 Tree-related (8)
19 Present (4)
21 Cultivated (5)
22 Sell illegally produced products (7)
24 It's the story of my life! (13)

DOWN

1 Speak lovingly (3)
2 Virgin martyr, patron saint of music, killed c. AD 230 (7)
3 Species of duck (4)
4 Blue dye (6)
5 Not the main event (8)
6 (Fire)place (5)
7 Information (9)
10 Lost again (anag) — hankering for the past (9)
12 Opener — Dr No book (anag) (8)
15 Coincide to some extent (7)
16 Hollow-stemmed tropical grass (6)
18 (Encourage)ment (5)
20 Serve a drink (4)
23 Rope used to secure a tent (3)

Solution see page 265

131

ACROSS

1 Decorative wall bracket for holding candles (6)

4 Offend (5)

7 Pure (like the Roman goddess of the hearth) (6)

8 Taking risks (6)

9 Stop (the flow) (4)

10 Framework (8)

12 Mull over (11)

17 Assertive — apt chime (anag) (8)

19 Adds up (4)

20 Implant (6)

21 Mythical Trojan hero during the siege by the Greeks (6)

22 Weighed down (5)

23 Be careful! (6)

DOWN

1 One not easily convinced (7)

2 Low piece of furniture with a hinged seat, forming a storage space (7)

3 Clamminess associated with fear (4,5)

4 Small glass bottle used for medical purposes (5)

5 Group of five (7)

6 Trim (6)

11 Awaiting developments? (9)

13 Contrary (7)

14 Insect's detector (7)

15 Wide part of a river as it nearsthe sea (7)

16 Unskilled — domestic servant (6)

18 1979 Ridley Scott sci-fi horror film (5)

Solution see page 265

132

ACROSS

1 Pay to get rid of (3,3)

4 Copy of a document on thin translucent paper (6)

9 Liquorice-flavoured Italian liqueur (7)

10 Stringed instrument instrument slightly larger than a violin (5)

11 Vault beneath a church (5)

12 Marine mammal with an ivory tusk (7)

13 King of the Franks and Holy Roman Emperor, d. 814 (11)

18 Cold north wind in southern France (7)

20 Bury (5)

22 Corn for grinding (5)

23 Shortage of rainfall (7)

24 Educational establishment (6)

25 Northern constellation, the Swan (6)

DOWN

1 Fundamentals (6)

2 Nice to eat (informal) (5)

3 Modest bet (7)

5 Prise (5)

6 Bird — hormone (anag) (7)

7 Every 12 months (6)

8 Tidy and pale (anag) — butterfly (7,4)

14 Cannabis (7)

15 Court-ordered divorce payment (7)

16 Mental representations (6)

17 Without charge (6)

19 Relative magnitudes of two quantities (5)

21 Attach (3,2)

Solution see page 265

133

ACROSS

1 Carnivorous plant (5,7)
9 Trembling poplar (5)
10 Cause to happen (7)
11 Churchgoer's assent? (4)
12 Southern California city, a major naval base (3,5)
14 Soft thin paper (6)
15 Deepest seated (6)
18 Go into the red (8)
20 Gelling agent used in foods, extracted from algae (4)
22 Oldest US university, established 1636 (7)
23 Language group that includes Swahili (5)
24 Easily understood (7,5)

DOWN

2 Female ruler (7)
3 Vases used for keeping ashes (4)
4 Concerning embryos in the later stages of pregnancy (6)
5 Submissive (8)
6 Wake up (5)
7 Absurd (12)
8 Disastrous (12)
13 Old instrument for measuring the altitude of heavenly bodies (8)
16 Material made of silk or a silk-like fabric (7)
17 Member of a Germanic people who ravaged Rome in 455 (6)
19 Too soon (5)
21 A son of Adam and Eve (4)

Solution see page 266

134

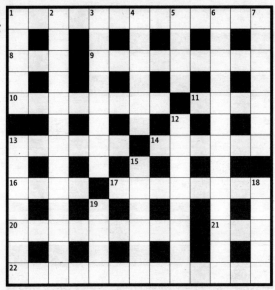

ACROSS

1 Lacking in courage (13)
8 As well (3)
9 Venomous snake (4,5)
10 First showing of a film (8)
11 Capital of Ukraine (4)
13 Befitting (6)
14 Breakfast food? (6)
16 Mass — volume (4)
17 Lift (8)
20 Properly in touch with the situation (2,3,4)
21 Impudence (3)
22 British naval hero, d.1805 (7,6)

DOWN

1 Nominate (3,2)
2 Eventually (6,2,5)
3 Asymmetrical (8)
4 Have enough money to buy (6)
5 Name of six Russian rulers (4)
6 Traditional beliefs, now discredited (3,5,5)
7 Become weak and die for lack of water (7)
12 Moby-Dick author (8)
13 Martial music played on the bagpipes (7)
15 Texas city on the Rio Grande (2,4)
18 North Yorkshire cathedral city with a racecourse (5)
19 Hit hard — run fast (4)

Solution see page 266

135

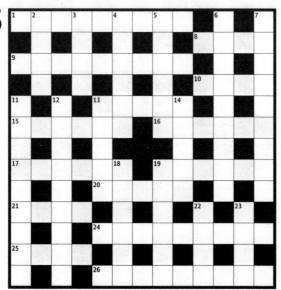

ACROSS

1 First meal (at Tiffany's?) (9)
8 Gentlewoman (4)
9 Greek equivalent of the Roman goddess Venus (9)
10 Furnace for firing bricks (4)
13 Neck and neck (5)
15 Iterate (6)
16 Gypsy (6)
17 Pluto, for example (6)
19 Cricketers' almanac (6)
20 Footwear (5)
21 Code word for G (4)
24 Very bright — sparkling (9)
25 Armoured fighting vehicle on caterpillar tracks (4)
26 Red food dye (9)

DOWN

2 Ecstatic — engrossed (4)
3 Israeli port city (4)
4 Gifted (anag) (6)
5 One posing for a portrait (6)
6 'Squashed fly' biscuit (9)
7 North Korean capital (9)
11 Spread widely — broadcast (9)
12 Atrocious (9)
13 Meres (5)
14 American world heavyweight boxing champion for 12 years, d. 1981 (5)
18 Most northerly town on the Scottish mainland (6)
19 Riches (6)
22 Write one's name (4)
23 Pavlova or Karenina (4)

Solution see page 266

136

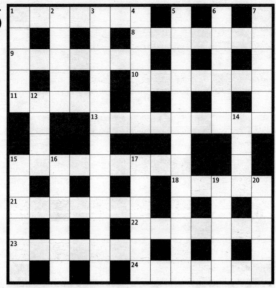

ACROSS

1 Diatribes (7)
8 Covered with hair (7)
9 Perfumed liquid (7)
10 Instrument for measuring electric current (7)
11 Body, excluding head, neck and limbs (5)
13 People living somewhere on a long-term basis (9)
15 Silvery metal found in bauxite (9)
18 Hard dark wood (5)
21 Short sharp knocks on a door (3-1-3)
22 Still proceeding as planned (2,5)
23 Firedog (7)
24 Look at (informal) (7)

DOWN

1 Implicitly understood (5)
2 Measuring stick with a straight edge (5)
3 World War II campaign to get people to grow food for themselves (3,3,7)
4 Clippers (6)
5 Peppermint-flavoured liqueur (5,2,6)
6 Main Irish stew ingredient (6)
7 Broken remains (6)
12 Semi-transparent gemstone, (4)
14 Urban area (4)
15 Safety device fitted in cars (3,3)
16 Messy (6)
17 Chant (6)
19 Nebraska's largest city (5)
20 Simple country cousin? (5)

Solution see page 266

137

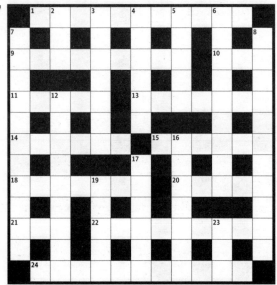

ACROSS

1 Be involved (11)
9 Lawyers (9)
10 Regret (3)
11 Chef's hat (5)
13 (Dis)coloured (7)
14 Makes fit for another purpose (6)
15 Less distinct (6)
18 Requiring little or no ironing (4-3)
20 Make reparation (5)
21 Sign of the zodiac (3)
22 Freelance photographers chasing celebs for a scoop (9)
24 About to happen (11)

DOWN

2 Gallery contents (3)
3 Great anguish (7)
4 Wensleydale, for example (6)
5 Rigatoni, tortellini etc (5)
6 Reservoir Dogs director (9)
7 Including qualities that are not attractive (5,3,3)
8 French armed police force (11)
12 Hunchback of Notre Dame (9)
16 A rag man (anag) (7)
17 Lacking foresight? (6)
19 Supply base (5)
23 Japanese school of Buddhism (3)

Solution see page 267

138

ACROSS

1 Parking system (3,3,7)
8 Play a leading role (4)
9 Continuing life routinely without much effort — cats go in (anag) (8)
10 Black Beauty author (4,6)
12 Noisy disturbance (6)
14 Deeply distressing (6)
15 Four-sided figures (10)
19 Boxer (8)
20 Be unsuccessful (4)
21 Risking everything (5,3,5)

DOWN

2 Radioactive element, Ac (8)
3 Major blood vessel (5)
4 Edicts (7)
5 Incensed (5)
6 Kneecap (7)
7 A parental sister (4)
11 Humorous verse form (8)
13 Serving (7)
14 Farm vehicle (7)
16 Principal (5)
17 Employee who runs errands (5)
18 Olympic sport similar to wrestling, developed in Japan (4)

Solution see page 267

139

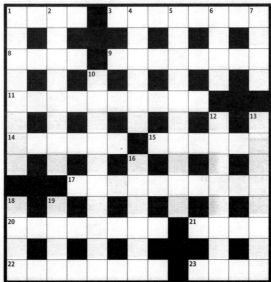

ACROSS

1 Command given to a trained dog (4)

3 Disagreements (8)

8 Coniferous tree (4)

9 Fearless (8)

11 Change (10)

14 Narcotic drug (6)

15 Social circle (6)

17 Custodians (10)

20 Sound made by a mobile phone (8)

21 Spun thread (4)

22 Retract (8)

23 Risqué (informal) (4)

DOWN

1 Seven-sided figure (8)

2 A genius! (8)

4 Congenital (6)

5 Publication appearing at regular intervals (10)

6 Certain sort (4)

7 Froth made from soap and water (4)

10 Drawn-out (10)

12 Computer security system designed to prevent attacks by crackers (8)

13 Bother (8)

16 Condition where an internal organ pushes through the abdominal wall (6)

18 Become bigger (4)

19 Nautical unit of speed (4)

Solution see page 267

140

ACROSS

1 Nominal leader (10)
7 Notorious (8)
8 Little devils! (4)
9 Swimming pool (4)
10 Lurch (7)
12 Hypothetical (11)
14 Pledge (7)
16 Device for making an electrical connection (4)
19 US coin (4)
20 Easy victory (8)
21 US singer and actor, born Dino Paul Crocetti, d. 1995 (4,6)

DOWN

1 Concluding (5)
2 Cause to be pleased (7)
3 Mob violence (4)
4 Hold back in making a decision (8)
5 Not getting any younger (5)
6 Attraction — legal process (6)
11 Porgy and Bess composer, d. 1937 (8)
12 Tight-fitting undergarment (6)
13 Exclude as a possibility (4,3)
15 Joint between two pieces of wood, forming a corner (5)
17 Gather — reap (5)
18 __ Fitzgerald, US singer, the Queen of Jazz, d.1996 (4)

Solution see page 267

141

ACROSS

1 Expert (4,6)
7 Be relevant (to) (7)
8 Luggage — lawsuits (5)
10 Require (4)
11 Ordinary person (8)
13 Mainland of Japan (6)
15 Gentle wind (6)
17 Ruler with absolute power (8)
18 Movable part of an aircraft's wing (4)
21 Revolting subject? (5)
22 Italian city — American smoked sausage (7)
23 Legendary marine monster (3,7)

DOWN

1 Prize money (5)
2 Kind of cormorant (4)
3 Trusted counsellor (6)
4 Deciduous tree — so creamy (anag) (8)
5 Petrol in France (7)
6 Unresolved (2,2,3,3)
9 Film script (10)
12 Fetters (8)
14 Eminent (7)
16 Gents' hairdresser (6)
19 Illumination (5)
20 Blackthorn fruit (4)

Solution see page 268

142

ACROSS

1 Teach (8)
5 Only — fair (4)
9 State of disgrace (5)
10 Hermit (7)
11 Inventor of the 'dambuster' bouncing bomb (6,6)
13 Urge on (6)
14 Looking glass (6)
17 Braggadocio (12)
20 Brought back to life (7)
21 France's longest river (5)
22 UK sea area west of Plymouth (4)
23 Small bright coloured beetle (8)

DOWN

1 Graven image (4)
2 Leaf vegetable (7)
3 Moneymaking (12)
4 Blood-red (6)
6 Common (5)
7 Government department conomy (8)
8 Now and then (12)
12 Three-headed dog guarding the entrance to Hades (8)
15 Italian composer of 39 operas, d. 1868 (7)
16 Arctic plain (6)
18 Heavy block on which hot metal is shaped by hammering (5)
19 Lifeless (4)

Solution see page 268

143

ACROSS

1 Persistent nuisance (4)

3 Curved sword (8)

9 Endurance (7)

10 Not a single person (2,3)

11 Biological units (5)

12 Hostility (6)

14 American homeopath, arrested for murdering his wife Cora and hanged in London 1910 (6,7)

17 Support for one who is lame (6)

19 Heraldic black (5)

22 Synthetic fabric, resembling silk (5)

23 Sudden increase (7)

24 Miscellaneous items (8)

25 So (4)

DOWN

1 Part of an address (8)

2 Temporise (5)

4 Royal residence on The Mall in London — cheer on, as clue (anag) (8,5)

5 (In music) note with a time value of half a whole note (5)

6 Old-time dance in duple time (3-4)

7 Smell offensively (4)

8 Complete disaster (6)

13 Numbers — steering (anag) (8)

15 Continue (5,2)

16 Be adamant (6)

18 Domingo, Pavarotti or Carreras? (5)

20 Nativity (5)

21 Greek god of love (4)

Solution see page 268

144

ACROSS

1 Cross and quarrelsome (9)
8 Lightweight crease-resistant synthetic fabric (5)
9 Emblem of royalty (7)
10 Woven fabric hung on walls (8)
11 Bushy hairstyle (4)
13 Norfolk seaside resort (6)
14 Chaste (anag) (6)
16 Rich soil (4)
17 Introduction (8)
19 Fabulous creature (7)
20 Animals found in a particular area (5)
21 Trip (9)

DOWN

1 Done (8)
2 Preposterous (6)
3 Genealogist's diagram (4)
4 Quite unexpectedly (3,2,3,4)
5 Speed up (4,2,3,3)
6 The art of gardening (12)
7 Person with an irrational urge to take things (12)
12 Liquid fuel (8)
15 Asian sultanate (6)
18 Fibre from coconut husks (4)

Solution see page 268

145

ACROSS

1 Modest and well-behaved (6)

4 Be plentiful (6)

8 Church council (5)

9 Transitory — death (7)

10 French dialect spoken in Belgium (7)

11 What's left at the bottom of the glass? (5)

12 Small cup — is steamed (anag) (9)

17 Hurled (5)

19 Modified to suit (7)

21 Ginger Rogers' 1930s' film dancing partner (7)

22 Cornwall's only cathedral city (5)

23 Way out (6)

24 Beasts (6)

DOWN

1 Repudiate (6)

2 Mixed (7)

3 Cowboy show (5)

5 Furthermore (7)

6 Merge (5)

7 Assimilate (literally and figuratively) (6)

9 Go through (9)

13 Cats (informal) (7)

14 Hand over for safekeeping (7)

15 Burning (6)

16 Detestable (6)

18 Express verbally (5)

20 On the move (5)

Solution see page 269

146

ACROSS

5 Style of neat round handwriting (11)
7 Implore (4)
8 Dearth (8)
9 Animate — breathe in (7)
11 Bedeck (5)
13 Signs of what's to come (5)
14 Small clump of trees (7)
16 Steadfast (8)
17 Jupiter (4)
18 Garden plant — re-do the pork (anag) (3-3,5)

DOWN

1 Nimble (4)
2 Spare time (7)
3 Satirical imitation (5)
4 Extinct mammal resembling an elephant (8)
5 Accurate clock (11)
6 Busy bee (5,6)
10 Gin-based cocktail with grenadine (4,4)
12 Gravestone inscription (7)
15 What's passed in a relay race (5)
17 Gag (4)

Solution see page 269

147

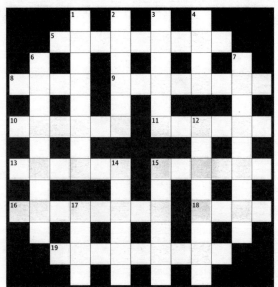

ACROSS

5 Hundredth anniversary (9)

8 Kind of credit card (4)

9 Hinged window (8)

10 Bequest (6)

11 More expensive (6)

13 __ Fisher (Beatrix Potter frog) (6)

15 Courageously — way to go? (6)

16 Arcane (8)

18 Make again (4)

19 Southern states that seceded from the US in 1861 (9)

DOWN

1 Walter ____ , English poet, d. 1956 (2,2,4)

2 Glutinous (6)

3 As new (6)

4 Forbidding (like the reaper?) (4)

6 Contrariwise (4,5)

7 Pause — delay (9)

12 Seductive (8)

14 Breed of terrier (informal) (6)

15 Fastening for a strap (6)

17 Barbershop procedure (4)

Solution see page 269

148

ACROSS

1 Movie (6,7)

8 Belgian (anag) — Asian language (7)

9 Sip or nibble, say (5)

10 Wrath (4)

11 North Sea (anag) — classic style of furniture (8)

13 Tarry (6)

14 Illegible handwriting (6)

17 Grabbed (8)

19 Not just a few (4)

21 Italian violin maker, d. 1684 (5)

22 Prevail — rejoice (7)

24 Issuer of parking tickets (7,6)

DOWN

1 Disorderly crowd (3)

2 Childish fit of anger (7)

3 Surrey County Cricket Club ground (4)

4 Unfortunate situation (6)

5 Eye disease (8)

6 Distressed (5)

7 For ever (9)

10 To begin with (3,1,5)

12 Naughtiness (8)

15 Frightened (7)

16 Very busy — fevered (6)

18 Philippine banana tree with leaf stalks used to make hemp (5)

20 Old Italian currency (4)

23 One of Attila's people? (3)

Solution see page 269

149

ACROSS

1 Lack of emotion or enthusiasm (6)
4 Praise — congratulations (5)
7 Small pampered pet (6)
8 Informal (6)
9 Quantity of paper, equal to 20 quires (4)
10 Angels of the first order (8)
12 Town in Fife, just north of the Firth of Forth (11)
17 Under an obligation (8)
19 Rotters (4)
20 Arrogant (informal) (6)
21 Writhe (6)
22 Aromatic herb (5)
23 Decapitate (6)

DOWN

1 Finished (2,2,3)
2 Midriff (7)
3 Fast (4-5)
4 Arboreal marsupial (5)
5 Eldest son of a French king and heir to the throne (7)
6 Biblical dancer, who demanded and got the head of John the Baptist (6)
11 Look back fondly (9)
13 Blue (7)
14 Encompass (7)
15 Tolerated (7)
16 Surprisingly brusque (6)
18 Thin and graceful (5)

Solution see page 270

150

ACROSS

1 Large edible plant of the parsley family — a glove (anag) (6)

4 Edgar Rice Burrough's Viscount Greystoke (6)

9 Mauna Loa or Stromboli, say (7)

10 Russian camp for political prisoners (5)

11 Straight lines from the centre to the perimeter of a circle (5)

12 Old timer? (7)

13 Turn the air blue (informal) (3,3,5)

18 Tiny margin — vibrissa (7)

20 Chocolate powder (5)

22 Provide sparingly (5)

23 Pewter pint pot? (7)

24 Very dirty place to live (6)

25 Long (boring) piece of writing (6)

DOWN

1 Significant others? (6)

2 Still legally binding (5)

3 Crunchy flavoured water ice (7)

5 Gas — organ (anag) (5)

6 Extremely large figure (7)

7 Trivial misgiving (6)

8 Unselfish — desecration (anag) (11)

14 Weak point (7)

15 Using few words (7)

16 Accepts responsibility (4,2)

17 Having real estate — came down (6)

19 No longer working (5)

21 Make sore by rubbing (5)

Solution see page 270

151

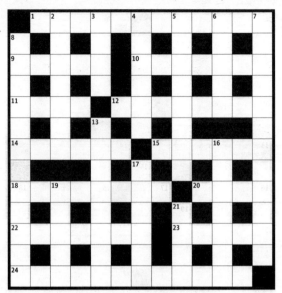

ACROSS

1 Otherworldliness — utility pairs (anag) (12)

9 Optical device producing an intense monochromatic beam of light (5)

10 Cowslip or oxlip, for example (7)

11 Cry (like a wolf?) (4)

12 Clerical robe (8)

14 Large Russian wolfhound (6)

15 A human 'tail' (6)

18 Appreciative (8)

20 Beloved (4)

22 Enthusiastic applause (often standing?) (7)

23 Member of an empire in Mexico, destroyed by Spanish conquistadors in 1515 (5)

24 Cross-country riding for pleasure (4,8)

DOWN

2 From August 1945? (4–3)

3 Uncommon (as hen's teeth?) (4)

4 Gave a gratuity (6)

5 Flight (8)

6 Harden (5)

7 Basic food additive in Marmite — exert tact, say (anag) (5,7)

8 A characterful broth? (8,4)

13 Pallet-raising truck (8)

16 Betray sexually (5,2)

17 Pear-shaped fruit used in jams and jellies (6)

19 One more time (5)

21 Flag (for a sailor?) (4)

Solution see page 270

152

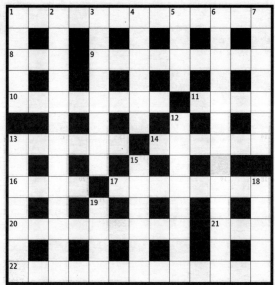

ACROSS

1 The Alps bug her (anag) — a kind of grapevine? (4,9)

8 Watering hole (3)

9 Getting too little remuneration (9)

10 Garden structure for keeping things (8)

11 Peru's largest city (4)

13 Atlantic bay stretching from Point Penmarc'h to Cape Ortegal (6)

14 Small basket of fruit (6)

16 Eurosceptic party, led by Nigel Farage 2006-09 and 2010-16 (4)

17 Extract from a dwarf citrus fruit used in Earl Grey tea (8)

20 Astaire or Rogers, for example (3,6)

21 Kind of whiskey (3)

22 Cause a complete reversal of circumstances (4,3,6)

DOWN

1 Constructed (5)

2 Dedicated tanner? (3,10)

3 Traditional weekday for UK general elections (8)

4 Climbing frame? (6)

5 Money transfer system via banks (4)

6 1, as opposed to I (6,7)

7 Water discharge pipe with a valve (7)

12 Balkan country on the Black Sea, bordering with Turkey (8)

13 Small Eurasian non-migratory bird with blue, yellow, white and green feathers (4,3)

15 Save (6)

18 Lock of a woman's hair (5)

19 Like lightning — don't eat (4)

Solution see page 270

153

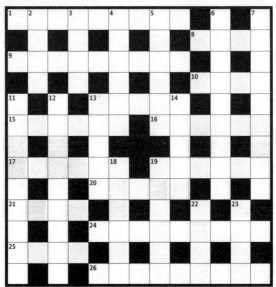

ACROSS

1 Garrulous (9)
8 Kind of chicken dish (4)
9 Bloom of youth (5,4)
10 Distinctive style or manner (4)
13 Hit hard (5)
15 Having an immediate impact (6)
16 Blue (6)
17 Bitter (6)
19 Announce (6)
20 Part of a device that goes round (5)
21 Set down carefully to a plan (4)
24 Boon (9)
25 Word that can be proper or common (4)
26 Sweet variety of plum (9)

DOWN

2 Just open (4)
3 Title given to important people like Genghis (4)
4 Very small (6)
5 Peeping Tom? (6)
6 Police department concerned with gambling, narcotics, pornography etc (4,5)
7 Pre-prepared for baking? (4-5)
11 Truly dreadful (9)
12 Done in a subtle, but harmful, way (9)
13 Seat for one (5)
14 Ferocious person (5)
18 Breed of vulture — no cord (anag) (6)
19 Respect shown publicly (6)
22 Antlered male (4)
23 Excited and curious (4)

Solution see page 271

154

ACROSS

1 Anxious and agitated? (2,1,4)
8 Provoked into action (7)
9 Become denser (7)
10 Journeying round a particular area (7)
11 Took a test again (5)
13 It's magic! (3,6)
15 Discombobulated (9)
18 Object for discussion (5)
21 Nonmetallic element used in integrated circuits (in a California valley?) (7)
22 Pardon (7)
23 Area near the wicket (7)
24 Different (7)

DOWN

1 Milan football club (5)
2 Not functioning properly (5)
3 Ridicule (4,3,6)
4 With no warmth (6)
5 Something enjoyed but not at once (8,5)
6 Moral principles (6)
7 (In music) slowly (6)
12 Bad (4)
14 An Asian cuisine (4)
15 Old fogey? (6)
16 Fill with optimism (6)
17 Kublai Khan's summer capital (6)
19 Rice flavoured with spices and cooked in stock (5)
20 Angler's basket for holding fish (5)

Solution see page 271

155

ACROSS

1 Instrument that records what's happening to the heart (11)

9 Something most eagerly sought or pursued — lily or hag (anag) (4,5)

10 Obtain for money — accept as true (3)

11 Adjust again (to zero) (5)

13 Straighten out (7)

14 Inessential, though desirable, item (6)

15 Hound (from Kabul?) (6)

18 Learned type (7)

20 One of 78 in a pack of cards (5)

21 (To a psychoanalyst) the conscious mind (3)

22 Unrestricted by reservations (9)

24 Little bits (11)

DOWN

2 Wholly (3)

3 Common name for Sirius (Alpha Canis Majoris) (3,4)

4 Unclear (6)

5 Fired up again (5)

6 HarperCollins or Simon & Schuster, say (9)

7 One of few final candidates (11)

8 Science of communications — cynic's beret (anag) (11)

12 Last two years of school classes (5,4)

16 Tiredness (7)

17 Squirm (6)

19 Abiding by the law (5)

23 Moved fast (3)

Solution see page 271

156

ACROSS

1 Very dark comedy (7,6)
8 Cosmetic powder (abbr) (4)
9 Wheel with projections on its rim that pull things through (8)
10 Playful primate (10)
12 Unprincipled (6)
14 Wild North American canine (6)
15 Game played with string looped over the fingers (4,6)
19 Composition for voices and orchestra based on a religious text (8)
20 Archbishop of Cape Town, 1986–96 (4)
21 Superciliousness (13)

DOWN

2 Taboo (8)
3 Temporary stand-in (5)
4 Sing carols from house to house (7)
5 Unit of frequency (5)
6 Absurd imitation (7)
7 Stringed instruments (abbr) (4)
11 Kind of woman's shoe (8)
13 Repeated aloud (7)
14 A High Wind in Jamaica? (7)
16 Units of an academic year (5)
17 Those against? (5)
18 Therefore (4)

Solution see page 271

157

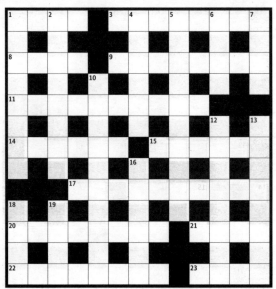

ACROSS

1 Travolta or Malkovich? (4)

3 Untrustworthy (3-5)

8 Sod (4)

9 Comedian (anag) — possessed (8)

11 Verging on the indecent — alien cited (anag) (10)

14 Dim (6)

15 Kind of edible oil (6)

17 Someone unable to relate to reality? (5,5)

20 Almond paste with egg whites (8)

21 Who knows who wrote it? (4)

22 Whizz-kid (informal) (2-6)

23 Vinegary (4)

DOWN

1 Throw away (8)

2 Transmission of genes (8)

4 Poor blighter (6)

5 Cabinet or shadow cabinet members (5,5)

6 Sharp blow (to one or other ear) (4)

7 Zero at Lord's or the Gabba (4)

10 Hotspot (10)

12 Mordant (8)

13 Decreed in advance (8)

16 You should try to avoid being in one of these! (6)

18 Complacent (4)

19 Rum and water (4)

Solution see page 272

158

ACROSS

1 Large tuba used in marching bands (10)

7 Vehicle seen between holes (4,4)

8 Make a loud animal noise (4)

9 German idealist philosopher, d. 1804 (4)

10 West Indian dance music (7)

12 UK's prerogative of mercy (5,6)

14 Wimp of a whiner (7)

16 Percussion instrument with acoustic chamber (4)

19 Elementary particle (4)

20 Boiler suits (8)

21 Narrow tube through which pellets are blown at a target (3–7)

DOWN

1 Standard — cattle (5)

2 No laughing matter! (7)

3 I'm afraid to say (4)

4 Will's Anne (8)

5 Anxious (5)

6 Clergyman (6)

11 Shifty dodger — bossy lot (anag) (8)

12 Curio (6)

13 Inactive (7)

15 Moulded ice cream dessert (5)

17 Middle-distance runner, like Roger Bannister or Hicham El Guerrouj (5)

18 O (4)

Solution see page 272

159

ACROSS

1 Paper strip once used in printers to record stock exchange prices (6,4)
7 Start to smoke (5,2)
8 Broth (anag) (5)
10 Friends and acquaintances (4)
11 One of a pair of upright posts — a dorm job (anag) (8)
13 Attraction (6)
15 Feudal subject (6)
17 Bribe (informal) (8)
18 Retained record of a payment by cheque (4)
21 Claw (5)
22 Self-centred person (7)
23 Not at all! (2,8)

DOWN

1 Miserly (5)
2 Quaint (4)
3 Engage (6)
4 Session of academic instruction (8)
5 Conceivably (7)
6 Bullet-proof vest (4,6)
9 Liquid or crystals added to foam and scent hot water (6,4)
12 Body established to settle disputes (8)
14 In the neighbourhood (7)
16 Inflammatory skin condition (6)
19 String (5)
20 Soya bean curd (4)

Solution see page 272

160

ACROSS

1 Still (8)

5 Multinational conglomerate that designs and sells ready-toassemble furniture (4)

9 Lover — fire (5)

10 Involving force (7)

11 16th-century Spanish adventurer in Mexico and Peru (12)

13 Gas, O (6)

14 Musical instrument consisting of a concave brass plate (6)

17 Book telling a story in pictures (7,5)

20 City hosting the annual Masters Tournament (7)

21 Group related by blood or marriage (5)

22 System of weights used for precious metals and gemstones (4)

23 With childlike credulity (4-4)

DOWN

1 Petty quarrel (4)

2 Analysis of the structure of animals (7)

3 Something (from Paris?) (7,5)

4 Without success (2,4)

6 Make (dough) uniform (5)

7 In the end (5,3)

8 Cautious (6-6)

12 Touching — Paignton (anag) (8)

15 The soul of wit? (7)

16 Musical interval of 12 semitones (6)

18 Bother (5)

19 Small drop (of sweat?) (4)

Solution see page 272

161

ACROSS

1 Forage crop with yellow flowers (4)

3 In the wings (8)

9 Fairy (7)

10 Bellini's 1831 opera (5)

11 Metal cast as a block (5)

12 He flew too close to the sun, fell into the Aegean and drowned (6)

14 Succeed by luck (3,3,7)

17 Related to the bony frame near the base of the spine (6)

19 Country run for 30 years by 'Papa Doc' Duvalier and his son, 'Baby Doc' (5)

22 Simulate (5)

23 From Tel Aviv? (7)

24 Variety of white wine first produced in the Rhine valley, now all over the world (8)

25 Hit hard with fist or bat (4)

DOWN

1 Cheap and inferior (8)

2 Fork part (5)

4 Fit in Uncle Joe (anag) — system for feeding internal-combustion engines (4,9)

5 He's busy over Christmas (5)

6 It can inflate or deflate (3,4)

7 Test (abbr) (4)

8 Grab (6)

13 Conspicuous — not at work (8)

15 Similar types (3,4)

16 Unit of Roman legion (6)

18 Gramophone record material (5)

20 Model of excellence (5)

21 A great distance away (4)

Solution see page 273

ACROSS

1 Spears eaten as a vegetable (9)

8 Taste of aged cheeses (5)

9 Manchester United player and French actor/director, b. 1966 (7)

10 Monster able to change appearance from human to wild animal and back again (8)

11 Fencing sword (4)

13 Account (6)

14 Chemical compound used as fertiliser (6)

16 Moored float (4)

17 Climbing plant with showy flowers — Islam etc (anag) (8)

19 Lenders at very high interest rates (7)

20 Shade of green (5)

21 Distant reaches of the physical universe (4,5)

DOWN

1 Sort of! (2,2,4)

2 Vegetables preserved in brine or vinegar (6)

3 Part of a ladder (4)

4 RAF officer rank (5,7)

5 Aside (5,7)

6 Going away from home base (7,5)

7 Butter, cheese etc (5,7)

12 Damage done to wood by burrowing larvae (8)

15 It became the 49th US state in 1959 (6)

18 Jupiter's Greek counterpart (4)

Solution see page 273

163

ACROSS

1 Feeling that one's been here before (4,2)
4 Exit (3,3)
8 Amalgamated (5)
9 Resolute and fearless (7)
10 100th of a Mexican peso (7)
11 Cause to perform again (5)
12 Desert (9)
17 First letter of the Greek alphabet (5)
19 Organic matter used as fuel (7)
21 Comprehensive (7)
22 Original New Zealander (5)
23 Uninspiring (6)
24 Sound of rushing air (6)

DOWN

1 Flaw (6)
2 Very recently (4,3)
3 Clear spirit (5)
5 Fish tanks (7)
6 Very unusual (5)
7 Hard to endure (6)
9 Contribute to the overall effort (2,4,3)
13 Kiss — £1 (7)
14 Spool, sticks and string game for one (7)
15 Inoculated (6)
16 8th century BC Hebrew prophet (6)
18 Flat — level (5)
20 Some welly! (5)

Solution see page 273

164

ACROSS

5 Making defamatory remarks (3–8)

7 Donkey's call (4)

8 (Of news) just coming in (8)

9 Set (7)

11 ___ Wallace, journalist and crime writer, d. Beverly Hills, 1932 (5)

13 Player (5)

14 Tangy Swiss cheese (7)

16 Altercation where claws are out? (8)

17 Envelop (4)

18 First US national park, 1872 (11)

DOWN

1 Nervous (4)

2 Drool (7)

3 Smile contemptuously (5)

4 In an evil way (8)

5 System where status has been earned (11)

6 On which military equipment is mounted (3,8)

10 Pedestrian evidence of the number shopping (8)

12 Objection (7)

15 Prod to do something (3,2)

17 Canine call (4)

Solution see page 273

165

ACROSS

5 From Montevideo? (9)

8 Prestidigitator's stick (4)

9 Senior official of the House of Lords (5,3)

10 Cultural environment in which something develops (6)

11 Vandalise (6)

13 Tiny swimmer (6)

15 Small mollusc (6)

16 Tour of watering holes? (3,5)

18 Somewhat (1,3)

19 Vehicle with large tyres for use on sand (4,5)

DOWN

1 American football playing field (8)

2 Holder for hens' products (6)

3 Deliberately misleading report (6)

4 Support (4)

6 Predatory (9)

7 Ceramic ware (9)

12 Spanish dance — a fond nag (anag) (8)

14 Ship used for deep-sea hunting (6)

15 Done by design (6)

17 Heart of the matter (4)

Solution see page 274

166

ACROSS

1 (In carpentry) an interlocking of tenons and mortises (8,5)
8 Loopy (7)
9 Device to hold things firmly together (5)
10 Faith, Hart-Davis or Smith? (4)
11 Common (8)
13 Kind of salad made with cos lettuce and croutons (6)
14 Suffer the consequences (of an action) (3,3)
17 Remedy (8)
19 With information (about) (2,2)
21 Swedish-born American film star, who wanted 'to be left alone', d. 1990 (5)
22 American film star, who said she was 'born at the age of twelve on an MGM lot', d. 1969 (7)
24 Sweetened Rhenish white wine (13)

DOWN

1 Knight (3)
2 Representing the best of its kind from the past (7)
3 At that time (4)
4 Slight (6)
5 Of the time of James I (8)
6 Saddam Hussein, for example (5)
7 Informal sort of cricket (3-3-3)
10 Gabriel or Raphael, for example (9)
12 Don't touch! (5,3)
15 Letters from admirers (3,4)
16 Symbol of infamy (6)
18 Cardinal number (5)
20 American high school dance (4)
23 Silly me! (3)

Solution see page 274

167

ACROSS

1 Help (6)

4 Harass (5)

7 Temple built as a pyramidal tower with an upward curving roof (6)

8 Pre-decimal 2 shilling coin (6)

9 Long hard march (4)

10 Native American chief supposed to have had a lover called Minnehaha (Laughing Water) (8)

12 Use of an inappropriate, though similar-sounding, word (11)

17 Kind of purple colour (8)

19 Posted (4)

20 Small ape (6)

21 Type of shed (4-2)

22 Particular (5)

23 Large black diving duck (6)

DOWN

1 Rearrangement of letters to form a new word (7)

2 Surface swimmer's tube (7)

3 Careless (4-5)

4 Under (5)

5 Continuous horizontal grey cloud (7)

6 Military helmet (informal) (3,3)

11 Relating to Jesus' 12 chief disciples (9)

13 Bitter in taste — harsh in tone (7)

14 Immediate — second (7)

15 Keep an eye on (7)

16 Put the phone down (4,2)

18 Nonsense (5)

Solution see page 274

168

ACROSS

1 Stitched up again (6)
4 In both directions (3-3)
9 Feeling one is about to fall (7)
10 Went by car (5)
11 Burn lightly (5)
12 Suspended freely (7)
13 Not convenient — trip up on one (anag) (11)
18 Punter hopes to hit it (7)
20 By tradition, the first Bishop of Rome (5)
22 Hard to swallow (5)
23 Gush (7)
24 Worked out (6)
25 Decorative band round the top of a wall (6)

DOWN

1 Charm — captivate (6)
2 Warning — she's a femme fatale (5)
3 Short report (5,2)
5 Make more extensive (5)
6 Made from sheep hair (7)
7 Supplies (6)
8 Talkative and rude (4-7)
14 Positively charged central core of an atom (7)
15 One giving wanted (or unwanted) betting advice (7)
16 Kicks out (6)
17 Doddle (6)
19 One due to get the money (5)
21 (Temporary) ceasefire (5)

Solution see page 274

169

ACROSS

1 Like Narcissus? (4–8)
9 Take place (5)
10 Seven-a-side team game — tall Ben (anag) (7)
11 Common sense (4)
12 It's set to cause future problems (4,4)
14 Picturesque (6)
15 Trouble (6)
18 On-the-spot treatment (5,3)
20 What one may do to teeth when one's angry (4)
22 Entrance (7)
23 (Hit someone on) the head (5)
24 They tell one where the wind is coming from (7,5)

DOWN

2 Bar (7)
3 Price paid to travel (4)
4 Clyde's associate (6)
5 Precisely (2,3,3)
6 What a performance! (5)
7 On purpose (12)
8 Differing perspectives — in spite of vow (anag) (6,2,4)
13 Diamond wedding anniversary (8)
16 Poirot's given name (7)
17 Mouth (informal) (6)
19 Dance music from Jamaica (5)
21 Most populous continent (4)

Solution see page 275

170

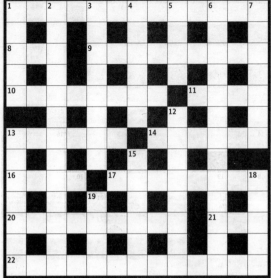

ACROSS

1 Person who manages the organisation (13)
8 Large vehicle (3)
9 Have a bash (4,2,1,2)
10 Sound of an incoming call (8)
11 High-quality — penalty (4)
13 It could be batwing, butterfly, leg-of-mutton or slit (6)
14 Dirty and/or poor-quality (6)
16 Container for flowers (4)
17 Black magic? (8)
20 Small balls fired together from a cannon (9)
21 Wood used for whisky barrels (3)
22 Crane fly — lands doggedly (anag) (5-8)

DOWN

1 Hard translucent fossil resin (5)
2 Get the wrong end of the stick (13)
3 Pessimistic (8)
4 Wise man (6)
5 ___ , Steam and Speed — The Great Western Railway (1844 Turner painting) (4)
6 Baked sausage dish (4-2-3-4)
7 Breeding colony for birds and also for seals and turtles (7)
12 Cost (5,3)
13 Attacked ferociously (7)
15 Will do (6)
18 I'm shocked! (5)
19 Depend (on) (4)

Solution see page 275

171

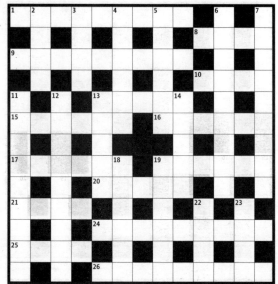

ACROSS

1 Absurd (9)

8 Inaction (4)

9 Act to reconcile differences (9)

10 Revise (at the last minute?) (4)

13 Watery component of blood (5)

15 Consecrate — order (6)

16 With added seasoning (6)

17 Expression of annoyance? (3-3)

19 Most senior (6)

20 Shabby (5)

21 Extremely — exact (4)

24 Open to interpretation (9)

25 Rocky outcrop (4)

26 Encouragement to a child who's taken a tumble (4-5)

DOWN

2 Limit (4)

3 Give out (4)

4 Millstone (6)

5 Kind of basic test (that turns red or blue) (6)

6 Intended (9)

7 Tax on a house purchase (5,4)

11 In an undertone (5,4)

12 Leading article — I tailored (anag) (9)

13 Cavity in the bones of the skull (5)

14 Truly, ___ , Deeply, 1990 Anthony Minghella film (5)

18 Join forces (4,2)

19 Peculiarity (6)

22 Lower house of the Russian Federal Assembly since 1993 (4)

23 Wiretaps (4)

Solution see page 275

172

ACROSS

1 Beer mug in the form of a 15 down man in a tricorne hat (4,3)

8 Model workplaces? (7)

9 Layered pasta dish (7)

10 Slope (7)

11 Erik ___ , French composer, who wrote five pieces he called 'furniture music', d. 1925 (5)

13 Payment made to copyright holders (9)

15 Flourished (9)

18 Increased (5)

21 Sat (an exam) for the second time (7)

22 Relating to physical reality (7)

23 Intellectually undemanding (7)

24 Describe (7)

DOWN

1 Negotiations (5)

2 Infatuate (5)

3 Funny business (7-6)

4 (Of film or photo) unclear (6)

5 A hand-held weapon? (7-6)

6 North America red deer — I paw it (anag) (6)

7 Weigh up (6)

12 Assert (4)

14 Rochester's Jane (4)

15 Stout (6)

16 Canadian city, founded in 1826, originally called Bytown (6)

17 Celebrity (6)

19 Town square (5)

20 Trick — duck (5)

Solution see page 275

173

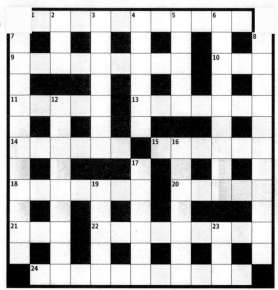

ACROSS

1 Plant-eating (11)
9 Girlfriend (9)
10 US actress MacGraw or Scottish writer Smith? (3)
11 Mediocre journalists? (5)
13 Commitment (7)
14 Figures of speech (6)
15 Ancient manuscripts (6)
18 Superhuman (7)
20 Tiny gnat (5)
21 Language closely related to Thai (3)
22 Trickle through — cereal pot (anag) (9)
24 Teenage years (11)

DOWN

2 Historical period (3)
3 Bloom (7)
4 Able to succeed (6)
5 All set (5)
6 Pure (9)
7 Berkeley Square serenader (11)
8 I yell drivel (anag) — lacking courage (4-7)
12 Pre-teenage years (9)
16 Opening in clothing (7)
17 Suit — Edinburgh football club (6)
19 Drive on (5)
23 Story line (3)

Solution see page 276

174

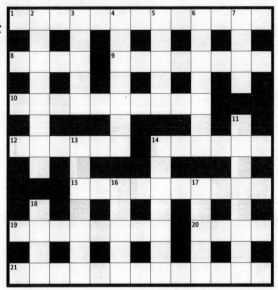

ACROSS

1 It has good and bad sides (5,8)
8 Strike (a toe) against an object (4)
9 Set of bells in a tower (8)
10 One with three siblings (10)
12 Transport for the departed (6)
14 Brimmed hat with an indented crown (6)
15 Source of stimulation (not instant!) (6,4)
19 Abrasive scourer (4,4)
20 Neighbourhood (4)
21 Human — family (5,3,5)

DOWN

2 Gatecrasher (8)
3 Implant (5)
4 ___ the Night, 1978 Bruce Springsteen and Patti Smith song (7)
5 Sign up (5)
6 Paid tribute to (7)
7 Gas used in illuminated signs (4)
11 An O'Brien (anag) — English composer, record producer and theorist, b. 1948 (5,3)
13 Bone disorder caused by vitamin D deficiency (7)
14 Stoked (7)
16 Plant life (in a particular 20) (5)
17 Scrap (5)
18 Setting control (4)

Solution see page 276

175

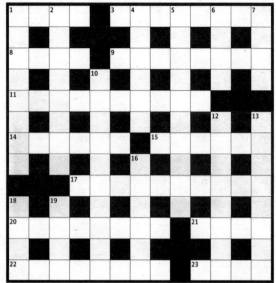

ACROSS

1 Fire (4)
3 Sharp-sighted (4-4)
8 Old-fashioned chap? (4)
9 Athlete involved in a gripping contest (8)
11 Cue reports (anag) — he's a bully (10)
14 Cleans — surgical gear (6)
15 Refer to indirectly (6)
17 Explosion on the sun's surface (5,5)
20 Suitable (8)
21 Latvia's capital (4)
22 Shy (8)
23 Cowshed (4)

DOWN

1 Useful pointer for motorists? (8)
2 Opposite (8)
4 Central area in a building, open to the sky (6)
5 It could trigger a revival (4,2,4)
6 Shout (4)
7 Mend with a needle (4)
10 Program for accessing the internet (3,7)
12 Daring (8)
13 Representative (8)
16 Secure (6)
18 Just the two (4)
19 Identify — location (4)

Solution see page 276

176

ACROSS

1 Deceptive — artful nude (anag) (10)

7 Practice (5,3)

8 Change direction suddenly (4)

9 Dip in liquid (4)

10 Of no help to anyone (7)

12 Psychic (11)

14 Legendary creature — I'm armed (anag) (7)

16 Weakling (informal) (4)

19 Fibre-rich byproduct of flour milling (4)

20 Distinctive flag (8)

21 Highway feature to stop livestock straying (6,4)

DOWN

1 Discovered (5)

2 Colourless, acrid-smelling gas, NH3 (7)

3 Fraught with danger (4)

4 The odds are stacked against it succeeding (4,4)

5 Belly button (5)

6 Rented room where you live and sleep (6)

11 Toy railway (5,3)

12 Thank you (informal) (6)

13 In bits (7)

15 Craze (5)

17 Rip up (5)

18 Panto part (like Judi Dench, perhaps?) (4)

Solution see page 276

177

ACROSS

1 Very softly (10)
7 Continues to irritate (7)
8 Easily understandable (5)
10 Type of sediment (4)
11 Gut feeling (8)
13 The ___ Man, 1973 horror film, starring Edward Woodward (6)
15 Earnest request (6)
17 Highly toxic soft metal, Tl (8)
18 Indian flatbread, cooked on a griddle (4)
21 Relating to a person (5)
22 Capital of French Guiana (7)
23 Crisp rolled gingerbread wafer, filled with cream (6,4)

DOWN

1 Expert assembly (5)
2 Supporter (4)
3 Crazy (6)
4 Beneficial (8)
5 Fake East London accent (7)
6 Personal timepiece (5,5)
9 Controlled — firm (10)
12 Sheets etc (3,5)
14 Appealing character (7)
16 Chorus of disapproval (6)
19 Accept personal responsibility (3,2)
20 Primary colour for printers (4)

Solution see page 277

ACROSS

1 Unthreatening (8)
5 Reverse (4)
9 Get punished (3,2)
10 Proportionately (3,4)
11 Long prison term (4,8)
13 It's up for debate (6)
14 Strong effect (6)
17 High fashion (5,7)
20 Come after (7)
21 Religion is 'the ___ of the people' (Karl Marx) (5)
22 Severe respiratory disease, first identified in 2003 (4)
23 Logically sound (8)

DOWN

1 Bumpkin (4)
2 Not a first edition (7)
3 Means of getting into correspondence (6,6)
4 Evening meal (6)
6 Adapt one's behaviour in the light of experience (5)
7 Reproductive organ in the human uterus (8)
8 Put on costume (anag) — showing disdain (12)
12 Extra stress (8)
15 Call before a court to answer an indictment (7)
16 Cook in hot (not boiling) water (6)
18 Slow-healing sore (5)
19 In the thick of (4)

Solution see page 277

179

ACROSS

1 Audacious (4)
3 Cordial (8)
9 Keen to find out (7)
10 Long-handled broom made of twigs (5)
11 At right angles to a ship (5)
12 Chinwag (abbr) (6)
14 Configuration of stars as seen from Earth (13)
17 Angle formed by the junction of two branches of a tree (6)
19 Get it down you! (3,2)
22 Device used to invert an image (5)
23 Unsophisticated young woman (7)
24 Go here in disgrace (8)
25 Checks closely (4)

DOWN

1 As luck would have it (2,6)
2 Syd Little's old partner (5)
4 Children's game that leaves one standing! (7,6)
5 A floating bedroom? (5)
6 Type of long-grained rice (7)
7 US television award (4)
8 Clever remark (3,3)
13 Snatches (8)
15 Nightingale's calling? (7)
16 Get even (6)
18 Pace (5)
20 Slight trace of colour (5)
21 Imitated in every way (4)

Solution see page 277

180

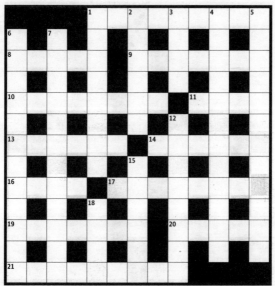

ACROSS

1 Made a positive impact (9)
8 Stand (5)
9 Sozzled (informal) (7)
10 Take to one's heels (4,4)
11 Pirouette (4)
13 Standing (6)
14 Stop messing about! (6)
16 Electric power cord (4)
17 Person who has a view (8)
19 Solvent used in nail polish remover (7)
20 Article of faith (5)
21 Act provocatively (9)

DOWN

1 Defining character of a person (8)
2 Stop at the roadside (4,2)
3 Advance cautiously (4)
4 Unconscious movement? (12)
5 Break up — sat re-editing (anag) (12)
6 Unemotional (6-2-4)
7 Reprint seems (anag) — to give an inaccurate account (12)
12 One forced to leave the country (8)
15 ___ Carter, novelist, short story writer and poet, d. 1992 (6)
18 Black eye make-up (4)

Solution see page 277

181

ACROSS

1 Soldiers' defensive ditch (6)
4 Outer part of a loaf of bread (6)
8 Light between red and green (5)
9 Give the wrong impression (7)
10 Dark-red sour cherry (7)
11 Atlas or Prometheus, for instance (5)
12 Go too far (9)
17 Begin to do something energetically (3,2)
19 Sharp front tooth (7)
21 Ear (informal) (7)
22 Short — essential information (5)
23 One suffering for their beliefs (6)
24 Dazed and confused (6)

DOWN

1 Emotional shock with lasting effects (6)
2 Agreement not to publish material before a certain time or date (7)
3 Yuletide song (5)
5 Italian rice dish cooked gradually in stock (7)
6 Used time (in a specific way) (5)
7 Section of rail track used for shunting (6)
9 Homes in on (anag) — illicit alcohol (9)
13 The environment as it relates to living things (7)
14 Posing a challenge (7)
15 Place of safety (6)
16 Artful (6)
18 The ___ Who Came to Tea, 1968 children's book by Judith Kerr (5)
20 Highland Games equipment (5)

Solution see page 278

182

ACROSS

5 Unpleasant clash (11)
7 Air pollution common in big cities (4)
8 Post holder (8)
9 MC on stage and screen (7)
11 Bishop's hat (5)
13 Confused (by life afloat?) (2,3)
14 Term of endearment (3,4)
16 Small stirrer — not Aesop! (anag) (8)
17 Make a reservation (4)
18 Nicest peers (anag) — tenacious behaviour (11)

DOWN

1 Hitch (4)
2 Outstanding amount to pay (7)
3 Where to write notes, musically (5)
4 Water-based paint (8)
5 What's left to rot in a garden (7,4)
6 Put one image over another (11)
10 (Exert) force (8)
12 A paltry sum of money (informal) (7)
15 It's uplifting (5)
17 Like a skeleton (4)

Solution see page 278

183

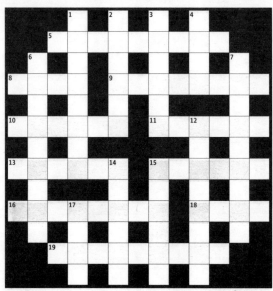

ACROSS

5 Performer's way in (5,4)
8 (Old) custom (4)
9 A Fellini? (anag) — it's at at your fingertips! (4,4)
10 Calms (6)
11 Fat from suet — two all (anag) (6)
13 Moved back and forth (6)
15 Groupings of similar things (6)
16 Definitely not for public consumption! (8)
18 Frost on things in the open (4)
19 Inform — educate (9)

DOWN

1 Works of art often put on a pedestal (8)
2 They act for others (6)
3 Something's got one hooked (6)
4 One of four on a horse, say (4)
6 Fan base (9)
7 Diagram showing room layout (5,4)
12 Sound of being tickled (8)
14 City on the Liffey (6)
15 Place providing pre-school childcare (6)
17 Cooked and ready to eat (4)

Solution see page 278

184

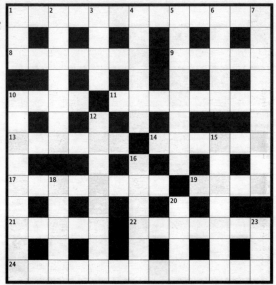

ACROSS

1 Unable to be put into words (13)

8 Overabundance (7)

9 Old French province in the Loire valley, an English possession from 1154 to 1204 (5)

10 Handle roughly (4)

11 List of times at which things are supposed to happen (8)

13 Unflinching (6)

14 Mexican mural painter, married five times (twice to Frida Kahlo), d. 1957 (6)

17 Without it, things are uneventful (8)

19 Left at sea (4)

21 Senseless (5)

22 Inspection (by house-hunters?) (7)

24 Take advantage of an activity that someone else started (3,2,2,3,3)

DOWN

1 ___ and outs (3)

2 In transit (2,5)

3 Nobleman (or woman) (4)

4 Tempt (6)

5 Cut of pork, often barbecued (8)

6 Small but elegant (5)

7 High-spirited (9)

10 Sense of apprehension (9)

12 Club — hit (8)

15 Unusual items (7)

16 Good in parts (6)

18 Repetitive song (by football fans?) (5)

20 College teaching industrial skills and applied sciences (abbr) (4)

23 Understand (3)

Solution see page 278

185

ACROSS

1 Send-up (6)

4 Cut meat, stone or wood (5)

7 Coming together of businesses (6)

8 Slender and graceful (6)

9 One gets over it as one gets older (4)

10 Underground energy source (4,4)

12 Regains Mali (anag) — place on the sidelines (11)

17 And so on (2,6)

19 Debatable (4)

20 Support for photography (6)

21 Line around an area to prevent entry (6)

22 Object used in playing chess (5)

23 Mixture of things from different sources (6)

DOWN

1 Extra cost (7)

2 One often found in pub? (7)

3 Order issued from above (9)

4 Nit-pick (5)

5 Recovers in health or morale (7)

6 Time for a mid-morning something? (6)

11 Sudden appearance of an overwhelming mass (9)

13 Record store (7)

14 Degenerate (7)

15 Thrift (7)

16 Repressed (4-2)

18 Common theme (5)

Solution see page 279

186

ACROSS

1 German state capital (6)
4 Cumin, cardamom etc (6)
9 Mexican liquor (7)
10 'Bloody Mary' was one (5)
11 Array of data in rows and columns (5)
12 Jailbird (7)
13 Log in stream (anag) — venomous lizard (4,7)
18 Eat rump (anag) — Japanese dish (7)
20 Teach (5)
22 Small boat (5)
23 Ardent (7)
24 Somnolent (6)
25 Far from obese (6)

DOWN

1 Undergo genetic change (6)
2 Muslim face veil (5)
3 Impossible fancy (7)
5 Don (3,2)
6 Common painkiller (7)
7 Parallel layers of material arranged one on top of another (6)
8 Don Quixote's squire (6,5)
14 Ginormous (7)
15 Reversal (7)
16 Kindling material — remote rural areas (6)
17 Playful (6)
19 Consume (3,2)
21 Botanical barb (5)

Solution see page 279

187

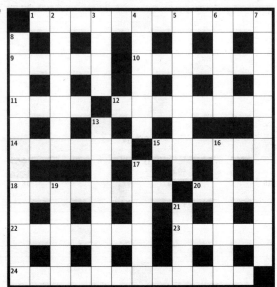

ACROSS

1 Lucrative enterprise (5-7)
9 Council tax (5)
10 Disproved (7)
11 Headland (4)
12 Passageway (8)
14 Sway, as if about to fall (6)
15 Part of the eye (6)
18 Magnified (8)
20 Solid scum on molten metal (4)
22 Detestable (7)
23 Happen (5)
24 Active Mexican volcano — top poet place (anag) (12)

DOWN

2 Eightfold (7)
3 Gaelic (4)
4 To some extent (4,2)
5 Told (8)
6 Eminent (5)
7 Author of She (5,7)
8 Forcibly assert authority (5,3,4)
13 Marvellous! (8)
16 Contrary to accepted morality (7)
17 Small projectile (6)
19 Reduction in intensity (informal) (3-2)
21 UK food retailing business (2-2)

Solution see page 279

188

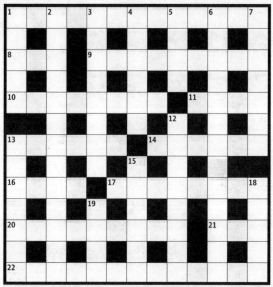

ACROSS

1 Welsh county (13)

8 High velocity weapon (3)

9 Hors d'oeuvre of sliced raw meat or fish (9)

10 Scratchy — harsh (8)

11 Not in favour (of) (4)

13 Blistering (3–3)

14 Roman army unit (6)

16 German organist and composer, d. 1750 (4)

17 Goodbye (8)

20 French national flag (9)

21 Curve (3)

22 Hard smooth-textured dairy product (7,6)

DOWN

1 Molten rock in the earth's crust (5)

2 Having no useful outcome (13)

3 Time — special event (8)

4 Prosper (6)

5 Sir Joseph ___ , light bulb pioneer, d. 1914 (4)

6 Lacking regard for the feelings of others (13)

7 Coastal problem? (7)

12 Systematic investigation to establish facts (8)

13 Unthinking, like a machine (7)

15 Courage in battle (6)

18 English empirical philosopher (the 'Father of Liberalism'), d. 1704 (5)

19 Ship's cargo-carrying space (4)

Solution see page 279

189

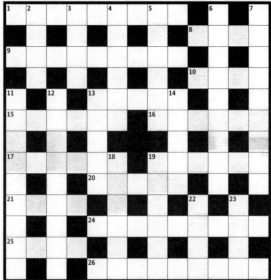

ACROSS

1 Calibrate (anag) — from bugs (9)
8 Cougar (4)
9 Motor race (5,4)
10 Smelly (4)
13 Film of oil on water (5)
15 Barely contain one's anger (6)
16 Rubbed out (6)
17 Loose from moorings (6)
19 Result (anag) — long loose overcoat (6)
20 Spin round (5)
21 Moussaka ingredient (4)
24 Oddly (9)
25 Figure in an emergency number (4)
26 Trio (9)

DOWN

2 Askew (4)
3 Just a suggestion (4)
4 Small disturbance on water (6)
5 Each one (6)
6 Something unusual (that can kill a cat?) (9)
7 Thick-skinned beast (9)
11 Invader (9)
12 Rebuke (9)
13 Rotating rod — ray of light (5)
14 Food for whales (5)
18 Spasmodic muscle contraction (6)
19 Suave (6)
22 Clutch components? (4)
23 Slight (4)

Solution see page 280

190

ACROSS

1 Protection from the sun? (7)

8 Fashionable (1,2,4)

9 (Of food) grown or raised naturally (7)

10 Violent stream (7)

11 Small fry (5)

13 Together — performing live (2,7)

15 Brahms and Liszt, say (9)

18 Tremble (5)

21 Attribute (7)

22 Eastern (anag) — resembling most closely (7)

23 Strong English accents (7)

24 Protective outer garment (7)

DOWN

1 Gambits (5)

2 Message understood! (5)

3 Holier-than-thou (13)

4 Derived from milk (6)

5 Honestly (4,3,6)

6 The Sailor Man? (6)

7 Shove off! (4,2)

12 Game played on horseback (4)

14 Music genre of the 1950s (4)

15 Cantankerous (6)

16 Very small metric unit of length (6)

17 Nevertheless (4,2)

19 Stadium (5)

20 Eulogise (5)

Solution see page 280

191

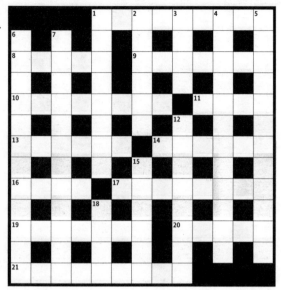

ACROSS

1 Cutting — snide (9)

8 River estuary between Argentina and Uruguay (5)

9 Overall chief (7)

10 Inca raid (anag) — it's a combination of industrial gas emissions with water in the atmosphere (4,4)

11 Touch with the lips (4)

13 Sea journey (6)

14 Jinx (6)

16 Stolen goods (4)

17 One from the island where Napoleon Bonaparte was born (8)

19 Marked with blotches (7)

20 Aquatic mammal that lives in a holt (5)

21 Requiring great exertion (9)

DOWN

1 Historically, the cheapest accommodation on a 13 (8)

2 Countrified (6)

3 Mountains of south-central Europe (4)

4 Chicago (3,5,4)

5 Type of running race (5,7)

6 Convey a great deal without using words (5,7)

7 GP (6,6)

12 North African dish of steamed semolina with a stew (8)

15 Family car manufactured by Ford since 1993 (6)

18 'A man, a ___ , a canal: Panama!' (4)

Solution see page 280

192

ACROSS

1 Voice sells lot (anag) — professional name of Declan Patrick McManus (5,8)

8 Formerly (4)

9 Bee-keeping locations (8)

10 Torch (10)

12 Unpretentious (6)

14 Recess (6)

15 Early anaesthetic (10)

19 Left stranded (8)

20 Part of the body between ribs and hip bone (often girded!) (4)

21 Troublesome possession (5,8)

DOWN

2 Floor covering (8)

3 Thoughts (5)

4 Code word for C (7)

5 Jazz style popularised in the 1940s (5)

6 Mercurial (7)

7 Porkies (4)

11 Repugnance (8)

13 Withdraw from a commitment (4,3)

14 Big read (anag) — shorten a text (7)

16 Cavalry weapon (5)

17 Muck (5)

18 Notes and coins (4)

Solution see page 280

193

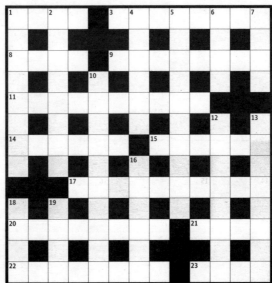

ACROSS

1 Moral evil (4)

3 Exaggerated masculinity (8)

8 Mixture of butter and flour used in cooking (4)

9 Chequer board game (8)

11 In difficulties (2,3,5)

14 Consequence (6)

15 Go red in the face (6)

17 Sunflower — lush in heat (anag) (10)

20 Colourless fruit brandy (3,2,3)

21 Yorkshire port city on the Humber (4)

22 Fletcher Christian, for example (8)

23 River Thames at Oxford (4)

DOWN

1 Morally good (8)

2 Titled lady (8)

4 ___ borealis (6)

5 Not able to go out (10)

6 Area of central London (4)

7 Depose (4)

10 Show Boat composer, d. 1945 (6,4)

12 Riding breeches (8)

13 Short stiff hairs (8)

16 Perceive intuitively — coming from God (6)

18 Cooperative group (4)

19 Bankrupt (informal) (4)

Solution see page 281

194

ACROSS

1 Cain's crime (10)

7 Prehistoric (8)

8 Unyielding (4)

9 Author of Das Kapital (4)

10 Daily record of events (7)

12 Formal and explicit approval (11)

14 First Soviet earth satellite, 1957 (7)

16 Strong restless desire (4)

19 Forehead (4)

20 Anti-British demonstration in Boston, Mass, 1773 (3,5)

21 Toasted Italian bread with a savoury topping (10)

DOWN

1 Arena for public debate (5)

2 Highly regarded (7)

3 Keep moving (4)

4 Battle that ended Bonnie Prince Charlie's Jacobite uprising of 1745–6 (8)

5 Postpone (5)

6 Chicken portion (6)

11 Theatrical performers (8)

12 Dab hand (6)

13 Pioneer American aviator, who disappeared with her navigator in the Pacific, 1937 (7)

15 Tall building (5)

17 Run scored at cricket but not off the bat (5)

18 Pedestrian way (4)

Solution see page 281

195

ACROSS

1 Italian cream cheese — co-spearman (anag) (10)

7 Beat soundly (7)

8 Subject (5)

10 Looked at (4)

11 Excessive action to achieve a goal (8)

13 Beat soundly (6)

15 Beat soundly (6)

17 Shocked (8)

18 Aspersion (4)

21 Four Quartets poet (5)

22 Beat soundly (7)

23 London rail terminus (10)

DOWN

1 North American elk (5)

2 Underwater vessels (4)

3 Reach one's destination (6)

4 JM Barrie's Boy Who Wouldn't Grow Up (5,3)

5 Relating to marriage (7)

6 Emphasise (10)

9 Night and Day songwriter (4,6)

12 Secluded (8)

14 Model — caliper (anag) (7)

16 The Great Stone Face, star of silent films, d. 1966 (6)

19 Tablecloth material (5)

20 Defensive ditch, usually filled with water (4)

Solution see page 281

196

ACROSS

1 Very hot day (8)
5 Bloke (4)
9 Frequently (5)
10 Goon era (anag)— herb (7)
11 Mixture of sodium bicarbonate and cream of tartar (6,6)
13 March to May in the southern hemisphere (6)
14 Prepared for publication (6)
17 MP's area (12)
20 Sickeningly obsequious (7)
21 The Gem State in the Rockies (5)
22 Bobcat (4)
23 Fearless (8)

DOWN

1 Shortly (4)
2 Pariah (7)
3 Christian rite — additional proof (12)
4 As much as necessary (6)
6 Picked up by the ears? (5)
7 Stick out (8)
8 Incredible (6,6)
12 Unrealistic (8)
15 Baroque keyboard composition (7)
16 Scattered (6)
18 Man-made fabric (5)
19 Affectionate (4)

Solution see page 281

197

ACROSS

1 Ostentatious ceremony (4)
3 Appraised (8)
9 Not connected to the internet (7)
10 Resentment of a slight (5)
11 Precise (5)
12 Four quarts (6)
14 Serving as an ordinary seaman in an old sailing ship (6,3,4)
17 Block of Earth's crust lifted to form peaks of a mountain range (6)
19 Card game (5)
22 Large commune of Rome at the mouth of the Tiber (5)
23 Non-attendance (7)
24 Hearth (8)
25 Conceited (4)

DOWN

1 Adages — Old Testament book (8)
2 Criminal organisation (5)
4 Legerdemain (7,2,4)
5 Evict (5)
6 Huge coniferous California trees (7)
7 Harts and hinds (4)
8 Speak at length about trivial matters (6)
13 First Minister of Scotland since 2014 (8)
15 Praise insincerely (7)
16 Uncover (6)
18 Leading performers (partnered with stripes?) (5)
20 East Africa country (5)
21 Code G (4)

Solution see page 282

198

ACROSS

1 Town in South Tyneside (6)
4 Handcart (6)
8 Momentary flash of light (5)
9 Reprimanded (7)
10 Leading (anag) (7)
11 Out of bed (5)
12 Communicate successfully (3,6)
17 Pulsate (5)
19 Satirise (7)
21 Having had careful prior consideration (7)
22 Manufacturer (5)
23 Constricted (6)
24 Soft tissue in bones (6)

DOWN

1 Puzzle with many pieces (6)
2 Bringing up (7)
3 Decide to participate (3,2)
5 Short-grain rice from Italy — or a biro (anag) (7)
6 Garden tools (5)
7 Walking through shallow water (6)
9 Mocked (9)
13 Chilli sauce (7)
14 Table game (7)
15 Filter — melody (6)
16 Scotland's patron saint (6)
18 Ohio or Delaware, say (5)
20 Venomous African snake (5)

Solution see page 282

199

ACROSS

5 Unfeeling (4-7)

7 Old (4)

8 Cud-chewing animal (8)

9 Companion and biographer of Samuel Johnson, d. 1795 (7)

11 Number of winks in a nap? (5)

13 Part of an act (5)

14 Groom's minder (4,3)

16 Informal photograph (8)

17 Gazpacho or gumbo, say (4)

18 Marine topic (anag) — curse (11)

DOWN

1 Did a runner (4)

2 Soon (7)

3 Third Greek letter (5)

4 Resist stubbornly (5,3)

5 Discerning experts (11)

6 Perfectly cooked (4,2,1,4)

10 Trachea (8)

12 Renault (anag) — state of gears when disengaged (7)

15 Beggar man's follower? (5)

17 Lingerie item — bit of paper (4)

Solution see page 282

200

ACROSS

5 About half a month (9)
8 Not yet up (4)
9 Embrocation for relieving muscular stiffness (8)
10 Spotted (6)
11 Something uncommon (6)
13 Looked after (6)
15 Very angry (6)
16 Cocktail served in a tall glass (8)
18 Dairy product (4)
19 Education (anag) — sold off (9)

DOWN

1 Flute, oboe etc (8)
2 Calm and unemotional (6)
3 Victor (6)
4 Buddy (4)
6 Former name of Ethiopia (9)
7 At once (9)
12 Call to mind (8)
14 Severe shortage (6)
15 Chap (6)
17 Quantity caught in a fishing net (4)

Solution see page 282

201

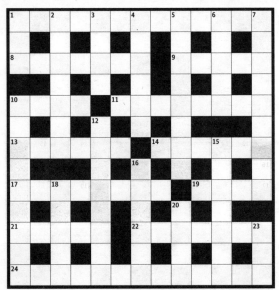

ACROSS

1 Fashionable 1950s' and 1960s' shoes (13)
8 Provide justification (for) (7)
9 Within the law (5)
10 Like a cucumber? (4)
11 Predicted (8)
13 Cosmetics (4-2)
14 South American cowboy (6)
17 Decreased (8)
19 __ Khayyam, Persian poet, d. 1131 (4)
21 Welsh dog (5)
22 Imprecise (7)
24 One old fort now (anag) (5,2,6)

DOWN

1 Fantastic! (3)
2 East Anglian county (7)
3 Pass water (informal) (4)
4 Snake (called Monty?) (6)
5 Blind alley (3-2-3)
6 Bird (that may be bald) (5)
7 Magnificence (9)
10 Involved with others in an offence (9)
12 Higher ranking (8)
15 Order (7)
16 Accepted doctrine (6)
18 Prison officer (slang) (5)
20 Zilch (4)
23 Light brown (3)

Solution see page 283

202

ACROSS

1 Type of hat (6)
4 Approximately (5)
7 Small bit of food (6)
8 Move up and down (6)
9 Play the Scottish game on ice (4)
10 Commonplace (8)
12 Acts of warfare (11)
17 Deep fissure (8)
19 Brusque (4)
20 Edible bivalve (6)
21 1960 musical with Bill and Nancy (6)
22 West Yorkshire city (5)
23 Freedom from danger (found in numbers?) (6)

DOWN

1 An excessive amount (3,4)
2 Slurs (7)
3 News reports (9)
4 Unimpeded (5)
5 What's left (7)
6 Without exception (6)
11 French novelist, writer of the 1898 open letter 'J'accuse, ... ' (5,4)
13 Watch and direct (7)
14 Tend (towards) (7)
15 Black magic (7)
16 Move through a web page (6)
18 Subjects of study (5)

Solution see page 283

203

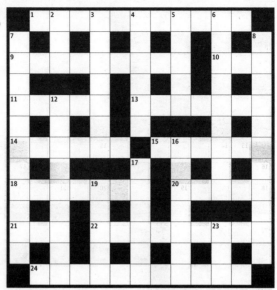

ACROSS

1 Type of needlework (5-6)
9 For the most part (2,3,4)
10 Observe (3)
11 Machine with more than one function (5)
13 Wheat, barley, oats etc (7)
14 Dutch royal house — fruit (6)
15 Fixed allowance (6)
18 V-shaped stripe (7)
20 Highest part in a piece of choral music (5)
21 Equipment (3)
22 Hold one's ground (5,4)
24 Fit to be seen in public (11)

DOWN

2 Codswallop (3)
3 Ostensible (7)
4 Not enough when compared with demand (6)
5 Deep — essential (5)
6 Stopping — canoeists (anag) (9)
7 Doddle (5,2,4)
8 Don's surname (anag) — aria from a Puccini opera (6,5)
12 Carnivore (4-5)
16 Pastoral paradise (home to the god Pan) (7)
17 To no avail (2,4)
19 Traditional Valentine's Day gift (5)
23 Ailing (3)

Solution see page 283

204

ACROSS

1 Source of caviar, found in the Black and Caspian seas (6)
4 Night biter? (3,3)
9 Nan (7)
10 Flat projection on the arm of an anchor (5)
11 Egg-shaped (5)
12 Row of leaping rugby forwards (4-3)
13 Absolutely ordinary (3,8)
18 Goat leather (7)
20 Longitudinal brace (5)
22 Little crown (5)
23 Pouch worn with the kilt (7)
24 Aide (6)
25 Fracas (6)

DOWN

1 Ringmaster's tent (3,3)
2 City from which the Dalai Lama fled into exile in India in 1959 (5)
3 Heathen (7)
5 Petite (5)
6 Lady's private room (7)
7 Deprived urban area (6)
8 Fingertip decorator (4,7)
14 Definitely unexpected (7)
15 Write (or leave) quickly (4,3)
16 Skit (6)
17 Cheeseparing (6)
19 Rascal (5)
21 Less well cooked (5)

Solution see page 283

205

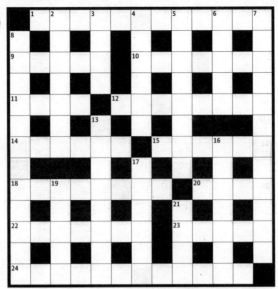

ACROSS

1 Glitz (6-6)
9 Sanctuary in the midst of strife (5)
10 Place for parking a boat (7)
11 Enthusiastic (4)
12 Breed of black-and-white cattle from northern Holland (8)
14 Satisfying meal (informal) (4-2)
15 Transparent (6)
18 Wrinkled (8)
20 Hairy Himalayan humanoid (4)
22 Nice area in France (7)
23 Soprano or tenor, say (5)
24 Large bunting (12)

DOWN

2 Inflamed swelling (7)
3 Outer part of citrus fruit peel (4)
4 Devon and Somerset national park (6)
5 Of hearing (8)
6 Former name of the Democratic Republic of the Congo (5)
7 Loco operator (6,6)
8 Group gathered to achieve a common goal (7,5)
13 Self-critical conscience (8)
16 Childish (7)
17 Come away (6)
19 Polite (5)
21 Female reproductive cell (4)

Solution see page 284

206

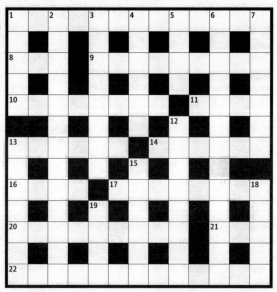

ACROSS

1 Belligerent (5–8)
8 Baby food catcher (3)
9 Jog the memory (4,1,4)
10 Metrical (8)
11 Classical portico (4)
13 Close shave (6)
14 Omani capital — white grape (6)
16 Large flightless birds (4)
17 Defamed (8)
20 Anonymous(ly) (9)
21 Prevail (3)
22 Uncontrolled competition for limited resources (7,6)

DOWN

1 Abstinent — muted in colour (5)
2 There you have it! (4,4,5)
3 Chap from this planet (8)
4 British Broadcasting Corporation? (6)
5 Kenneth Grahame's gentleman amphibian from The Wind in the Willows (4)
6 Human double (9,4)
7 Dashing and bold (7)
12 À bientôt! (2,6)
13 US arresting officer? (7)
15 Severe beating (6)
18 Pretty and neat (kind of old toy car?) (5)
19 Trademarked citrus fruit (4)

Solution see page 284

207

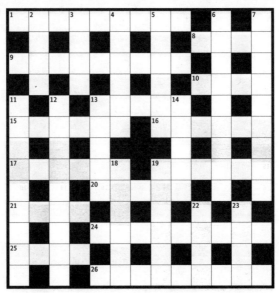

ACROSS

1 Triangular Russian instrument (9)

8 Hindu teacher who has achieved a high level of spiritual insight (4)

9 Deliberately make more confusing (9)

10 Computing unit (4)

13 Extremely cold — at the extremes (5)

15 American hotdog — ie wren (anag) (6)

16 Rodent — per hog (anag) (6)

17 Coniferous tree (6)

19 Scrooge (informal) (6)

20 Foot traveller who, for pleasure, goes on extended walks (5)

21 Weakest in the litter (4)

24 Causing excitement (9)

25 State of deep and prolonged unconsciousness (4)

26 Revelation (3-6)

DOWN

2 Swedish pop group, formed 1972 (4)

3 Chills and fever (4)

4 Tower of strength (6)

5 What holds a soldier's clothes and personal possessions (6)

6 Lightweight thermoplastic, used in packaging (9)

7 Extra food on a smaller plate (4,5)

11 Showing wonder and dread (9)

12 Musician's timekeeper (9)

13 Beauty — furry fruit (5)

14 Lunar exploration vehicle? (5)

18 Five sixteens (6)

19 Country where Guadalajara is to be found (6)

22 Stick(er) (4)

23 Initial contribution players make to the pot (4)

Solution see page 284

208

ACROSS

1 24 cutter (7)
8 Harmful look? (4,3)
9 Labour standard? (3,4)
10 Enlarge (7)
11 In progress (5)
13 Student of animal life (9)
15 Small boiled sweet (like a fairy?) — gulp as rum (anag) (9)
18 Saying widely assumed to be true (5)
21 Continue for too long (7)
22 Pistol, say (7)
23 Rain lightly (7)
24 Where doctors see their patients (7)

DOWN

1 Bashar al–Assad's country (5)
2 Sound part of a transmitted signal (5)
3 Annual award for journalism, literature, musical composition and public service, established 1917 (8,5)
4 (Musically) smooth (6)
5 RAF officer (4,9)
6 From Saudi Arabia's southern neighbour? (6)
7 Musical composition for seven performers (6)
12 German woman (4)
14 Grain tower (4)
15 Unethical — dishonest (6)
16 A Celtic language (6)
17 Transparent optical devices (6)
19 Spitting blood (or feathers) (5)
20 Ancient Egyptian kept under wraps (5)

Solution see page 284

209

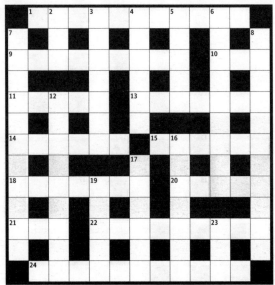

ACROSS

1 Truth disguised as a lie (or vice versa) (6,5)
9 Is incompatible (with) (9)
10 Scamp (3)
11 Bingo (5)
13 During the first stages (5,2)
14 Thickset (6)
15 Keep back (6)
18 Non-believer (7)
20 Estimate — shot (5)
21 And so on (abbr) (3)
22 Unrehearsed (9)
24 1st of 365 (or 366) (3,5,3)

DOWN

2 Belonging to a specified person (3)
3 Young (or castrated) male bovine (7)
4 Surpass (6)
5 Unsuccessful gambler (5)
6 Magical story with a happy ending (5,4)
7 Flat pastries filled with dried fruit — less EEC cack (anag) (6,5)
8 Completely straightforward (4-3-4)
12 Odontalgia (9)
16 Completely engage (7)
17 Completely ideal state (6)
19 In a frosty manner (5)
23 Pulse (3)

Solution see page 285

210

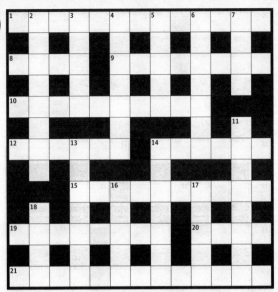

ACROSS

1 Unsheathe for a fight (4,4,5)
8 Get by wheedling (4)
9 Deep-fried minced meats coated in egg and breadcrumbs (8)
10 Person deprived of food (10)
12 Bird house (6)
14 Major boulevard of Beverly Hills and West Hollywood (6)
15 Smooth-textured Italian pork sausage — a dermal lot (anag) (10)
19 Nicked — stopped (8)
20 Fry or bake? (4)
21 Conduct of doctor to patient (7,6)

DOWN

2 One's own flesh and blood? (8)
3 Bet (5)
4 Place for fostering and promoting growth (7)
5 Cold rice balls with raw fish (5)
6 Bad egg (7)
7 Submerged ridge of rock or coral (4)
11 Very horrid place (8)
13 Melissa (anag) — with no clear purpose (7)
14 Fame (7)
16 Thought highly of (5)
17 Former prisoner (an old Tory?) (2–3)
18 French soft white cheese (4)

Solution see page 285

211

ACROSS

1 Pompous talk (4)

3 Embarrassed and lacking selfconfidence (8)

8 Skin spots (informal) (4)

9 Broad (8)

11 Breakfast cooker? (6,4)

14 Awkward and inexperienced youth (6)

15 Fixed number of lines forming a unit of a poem (6)

17 Device for freezing water (3,7)

20 Highest point (8)

21 Rend (4)

22 Think deeply (8)

23 Stage (4)

DOWN

1 Stock term rendered meaningless by endless repetition (8)

2 Catastrophe that cannot be insured against (3,2,3)

4 50th US state (6)

5 Visual communication? (3,7)

6 Long-legged wader (4)

7 __ and kisses (4)

10 Unaccompanied church music sung in unison — a ninth clap (anag) (10)

12 Circuitous (8)

13 Casually mention famous people you know to impress your audience (8)

16 Lucky charm (6)

18 Heroic and long (4)

19 Close-fitting (4)

Solution see page 285

212

ACROSS

1 Expressing disapproval (10)

7 Greek form of mandolin (8)

8 You — 1,000 (abbr) (4)

9 Rounded projection, part of a larger structure (4)

10 Georgia's capital (7)

12 Failure to work (11)

14 Founder member of the European Economic Community (7)

16 Brief falling out (4)

19 Hole (for a coin?) (4)

20 Smear — slander (8)

21 Dawn (5,2,3)

DOWN

1 Loiter with no apparent aim (5)

2 Shameless scheming woman (7)

3 Debauched elderly man (4)

4 Long traffic queue (8)

5 Absolutely essential (5)

6 US icon (anag) — indirect relation (6)

11 Residential district on a city's outskirts (8)

12 Breakfast food, originally developed by a Swiss doctor for his patients (6)

13 Tacit (7)

15 Amphibious reptile (abbr) (5)

17 Cheap and nasty (5)

18 European capital (4)

Solution see page 285

213

ACROSS

1 Rightfulness (10)
7 Alkali metal, Li (7)
8 Fizzing firework (5)
10 Weave — air in the lungs (4)
11 River that flows through the Grand Canyon (8)
13 Barked in a high-pitched tone (6)
15 Ally (6)
17 Tincture of opium — maul UN ad (anag) (8)
18 The H in GBH (4)
21 Blanched (5)
22 Window fitter (7)
23 Inexplicable (10)

DOWN

1 Reveal information (3,2)
2 Benefit (4)
3 Drum beaten with the hands (3-3)
4 Rising in the Rockies, the longest river in North America (8)
5 Ability to face danger (7)
6 Providing every detail (4-2-4)
9 Vodka and tomato juice, with some Worcester sauce (6,4)
12 Degenerate (8)
14 Deficiency (7)
16 Uncouth (6)
19 Awry (5)
20 Lower part of an inside wall, finished differently from the rest (4)

Solution see page 286

214

ACROSS

1 Communication mailed with no envelope (8)
5 A or the? (4)
9 Rule (5)
10 Approval (2-5)
11 Stick tipped with iron (12)
13 Very much (4,2)
14 Winter hanger-on? (6)
17 Amoral (12)
20 Simulate (7)
21 Out and away (2,3)
22 Roué (4)
23 Supplement at the end of a written work (8)

DOWN

1 Fringe benefit (abbr) (4)
2 Taking possession by force (7)
3 Two middle pages of a magazine (6,6)
4 Well-built and rough-looking (6)
6 Eighth letter in the Greek alphabet (5)
7 Adapted (8)
8 Controversial issue that's the talk of the town (5,7)
12 Odd (8)
15 Well pleased (informal) (7)
16 Financial support (6)
18 Simper (5)
19 Large African antelope with long straight horns (4)

Solution see page 286

215

ACROSS

1 Total admission revenue from a sporting event (4)

3 Common pest of gardens and crops (8)

9 Word of initials (7)

10 Greek author of fables, d. c. 560 BC (5)

11 I've no idea (informal) (5)

12 Viz (6)

14 Current astrological period (heyday of the hippie and NewAge movements?) (3,2,8)

17 Source of great authority (6)

19 Marinade used on meat in Indian cuisine before grilling in a clay oven (5)

22 Chide a child (5)

23 Automatons (7)

24 Pair of pincers (8)

25 Person who is the senior member of a group (4)

DOWN

1 Daily newspaper, founded 1821 in Manchester (8)

2 Italian city with a shroud (5)

4 Kitchen utensil kept busy on Pancake Day? (5,8)

5 Deep gap (5)

6 Spiral pasta (7)

7 Nervous tension on the putting green? (4)

8 Unique thing (3-3)

13 Hired murderer (8)

15 Aural aperture (7)

16 Keats's 'season of mists and mellow fruitfulness' (6)

18 Port where in 1587 Francis Drake 'singed the King of Spain's beard' (5)

20 Kevin ___ , American actor and singer, b. 1947 (5)

21 Listen! (4)

Solution see page 286

216

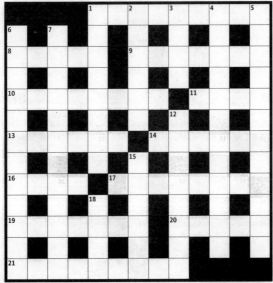

ACROSS

1 Kind of equation (9)
8 Commotion (3-2)
9 Pasta cushions with a savoury filling (7)
10 Slightly salty, with mixture of sea and fresh water (8)
11 In the same place (abbr) (4)
13 Termination (6)
14 Exhibitionist— rose up (anag) (6)
16 Thrill (4)
17 Poorly executed (8)
19 One removed from danger (7)
20 Leather strip (5)
21 Lead(er) (9)

DOWN

1 Duck talk? (8)
2 Kind of clue (6)
3 Talk in a noisy and excited way (4)
4 Analyse and solve problems (12)
5 Brilliant young talent (5,7)
6 Something wonderful (3,4,5)
7 Be a toady (3,3,6)
12 Vied (8)
15 Shirt part (6)
18 Throaty seductive sound (4)

Solution see page 286

217

ACROSS

1 Most quaint (6)
4 Old calculator (6)
8 A Balearic island (5)
9 Story set at an earlier time than is covered in a previous work (7)
10 Foolishly grand (7)
11 Years before reaching twenty (5)
12 Drambuie and Scotch cocktail (5,4)
17 Mountain ash (5)
19 Offensive (7)
21 Depth of a vessel's keel below the surface (7)
22 Dress (5)
23 Breathe out (6)
24 Australia's most populous city (6)

DOWN

1 Upbeat (as a bird?) (6)
2 Cutting device (7)
3 Military headgear with a peak and a plume (5)
5 Meaty drink (4,3)
6 Lacking in tact (5)
7 Spatter (6)
9 Equivocate (informal) (9)
13 West African country, capital Dakar (7)
14 Take a reclining position (3,4)
15 Kitchen cooler (6)
16 Fifty-two times a year (6)
18 Fury (5)
20 Weak and sentimental person (informal) (5)

Solution see page 287

218

ACROSS

5 High-quality wooden furniture (11)
7 Groucho or Karl? (4)
8 In the manner of a ruffian (8)
9 Chap with a carrot for a nose? (7)
11 Kind of dirty music? (5)
13 Weave into braids (5)
14 Well (7)
16 State in control over a subservient one — Iran/Suez (anag) (8)
17 Inverted stitch (4)
18 Squander (7,4)

DOWN

1 Mountain goat (4)
2 Detains (anag) — in lieu (7)
3 Fat — dark beer (5)
4 Silly comic verse (8)
5 Scan TV stations (7,4)
6 One version of Nelson's dying words (4,2,5)
10 Supposedly harmless fib (5,3)
12 Name for Mr Fox (7)
15 Matilda's dance (to Strauss's music?) (5)
17 Weakest chess piece (4)

Solution see page 287

219

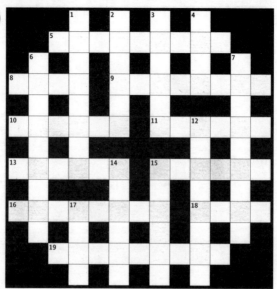

ACROSS

5 Insular (9)
8 Bowline or sheet bend? (4)
9 Winning — getting (8)
10 Garter, running or saddle? (6)
11 Country around Bergen (6)
13 Scanty (6)
15 Invite (6)
16 Unrefined petroleum (5,3)
18 Indian dress draped over shoulderor head (4)
19 Period determined by the moon's phases (5,4)

DOWN

1 Servant with many skills (8)
2 Dried vegetable sponge (6)
3 Bleach (6)
4 Potato dish (4)
6 Who wants it? (3,6)
7 Disagreeable (9)
12 Celebrated singer of a certain kind of music (4,4)
14 Old freeholder — one May (anag) (6)
15 Second of Henry VIII's six (6)
17 Beat easily (4)

Solution see page 287

220

ACROSS

1 Traditional plate of food (4,3,3,3)
8 One of a pair on a rail? (7)
9 River mouth, like that of the Nile (5)
10 Hit over the head? (4)
11 Hemisphere that includes North, Central and South America (3,5)
13 Remove the bones (6)
14 Decorative ball worn on a hat (6)
17 Dig up (8)
19 Portent (4)
21 Group of thirteen witches (5)
22 Participants in a violent disturbance of the peace (7)
24 Boris v Keir? (5,8)

DOWN

1 Computer — coat (3)
2 Substance under pressure released as a fine cloud (7)
3 Absent (with the fairies?) (4)
4 Ass (6)
5 Fine china and porcelain manufacturer, founded in Staffordshire in 1759 (8)
6 Yet more despicable (5)
7 Soldier in the Grenadiers? (9)
10 Espresso holder? (6,3)
12 Divine (8)
15 Ancient city buried by an eruption of Vesuvius (7)
16 Music player (6)
18 Person going underground for pleasure (5)
20 Desert of southern Mongolia and northern China (4)
23 Help! (3)

Solution see page 287

221

ACROSS

1 Unseat (6)

4 Replacement of what has been drunk from the glass (3-2)

7 Hot green condiment (6)

8 Large shapeless lump (6)

9 Pain in the eye? (4)

10 Smelling of strongly flavoured cloves (8)

12 On which wet smalls are hung (7,4)

17 It's best to avoid being in this (3,5)

19 Goodbye! (informal) (2-2)

20 Spliff (6)

21 Outdoor canopy (6)

22 Romantic rendezvous (5)

23 Bond (6)

DOWN

1 Extreme (7)

2 Dummy pill (7)

3 Catapult — night loss (anag) (9)

4 Internet pest (5)

5 Bird, whose 'beak can hold more than his belly can' (7)

6 Tropical melon-like fruit with yellowish flesh (6)

11 Appear again (9)

13 Something whose outcome is a chance event (7)

14 Acute (7)

15 Dead and gone (7)

16 Desire (6)

18 One acting for another (5)

Solution see page 288

222

ACROSS

1 Attention-seeking — showy (6)
4 Performing well (2,4)
9 Unnamed individual (2-3-2)
10 Fat — stout (5)
11 Top (5)
12 Obstinately resistant to change (3-4)
13 Paintings by Pollock or Kandinsky, say (8,3)
18 It may be blocked, flared or pierced (7)
20 Chekhov's Vanya's family status (5)
22 Come in (5)
23 Table linen (7)
24 Bring (or fall) down (6)
25 One adds fuel to the fire (6)

DOWN

1 Bringing together of separate elements (6)
2 Adjust to new circumstances (5)
3 Bolt-hole (7)
5 Hanging loop (5)
6 In opera (anag) — held outside (4-3)
7 Gluttonous (6)
8 Making unsolicited approaches to potential customers (4,7)
14 Passengers' waiting area (3,4)
15 Some may blow their own (7)
16 Discontent (6)
17 Person authorised to cut material deemed offensive (6)
19 Rustic (5)
21 Get on well (informal) (5)

Solution see page 288

223

ACROSS

1 Full of different events (6-6)
9 Fragrance (5)
10 Forces (7)
11 Intense satisfaction (informal) (4)
12 A matchless fellow? (8)
14 Run-of-the-mill (6)
15 Father Ted or Frasier? (6)
18 Good enough (8)
20 Mountain lake (4)
22 Conceive (7)
23 Disturbed (5)
24 It keeps drinks hot or cold (7,5)

DOWN

2 Better quality (7)
3 The terrible Russian? (4)
4 Raw material for honey (6)
5 Sitting room furniture (8)
6 Mourning ring? (5)
7 Notice the difference — iced martinis (anag)? (12)
8 It's much discussed (7,5)
13 Model (8)
16 Main supporting structure of a car (7)
17 Gripping tool (6)
19 Humiliation (5)
21 Scavenging seabird (4)

Solution see page 288

224

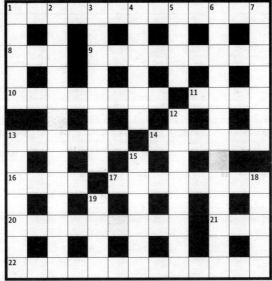

ACROSS

1 Recordings of popular songs (they're never original!) (5,8)

8 It goes with chicken (and bacon!) (3)

9 One engaged in mortal combat as entertainment in ancient Rome (9)

10 Driving hazard (8)

11 Anglo–Saxon king (with a dyke?) (4)

13 ___ Gray, young man pictured in Oscar Wilde's 1890 novella (6)

14 Fungal wood decay (3,3)

16 Rise rapidly (4)

17 Put forward (8)

20 State of something subjected to very high temperatures (5,4)

21 Category 4 Atlantic hurricane that hit Cuba and the US in August/ September (3)

22 Irish author of Waiting for Godot (6,7)

DOWN

1 Not costly (5)

2 Diet adopted by Leo Tolstoy and George Bernard Shaw (13)

3 To do with a particular part of the country (8)

4 Part of a tooth (6)

5 Read quickly (4)

6 Rusty — picture of a cot (anag) (3,2,8)

7 Retainer (7)

12 Relating to the meaning of words (8)

13 Repudiates (7)

15 It describes how something is done (6)

18 Rough initial version of a written work (5)

19 Small, long-haired dog (abbr) (4)

Solution see page 288

SOLUTIONS

1

```
S E P S I S · · S H A D O W
I · L · D · · · E · E · I
M A U V E · · C A L I B R E
O · N · A · H · I · A · N
N I G E L L A · · P U R S E
E · E · · M · A · · · · R
· · R I C E P A D D Y · ·
C · · · O · A · · · A · C
O C T E T · G A S C O N Y
R · O · E · N · P · U · P
T A X F R E E · L U N A R
E · I · I · · · I · D · U
Z O N K E D · · A T H E N S
```

2

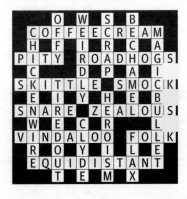

3

```
· · · B · P · F · B · ·
· V O R A C I O U S · ·
· B · N · N · L · S · V
G O S H · T E L E T H O N
· Y · O · R · I · · · U
S C U M M Y · P A U N C H
· O · I · · · · S · · H
S T R E A K · P L E A S E
· T · N · H · R · · · A
N E X T D O O R · N A F F
· D · O · T · A · A · E
· T O O T H S O M E · ·
· · · K · Y · E · E · ·
```

4

```
```

SOLUTIONS

5

```
H I J A C K   L O C U M
E   O   A     A   A   A
E N G U L F   R U N N E R
C   R   E     G   V   T
B O R N   T O P H E A V Y
O   A   I   I   S   R
  P O L T E R G E I S T
S   M   R   G   N   A
T R I C K E R Y   S I N K
A   N   N   B   U   N
R I O T E R   A L L I E D
V   U   L   N   I   R
E A S E L   S K I N N Y
```

6

```
C L U T C H   F L O W E R
H   P   O   A   I   A   E
E T E R N A L   L O Y A L
R   N   F   T   L   W   I
U N D U E   E L E V A T E
B   S   R   R       R   F
  O D D S A N D E N D S
V   E   A   N       N   C
E X P L O I T   A T S E A
R   L   L   I   B   P   R
S P E N D   V I L L A G E
U   T   E   E   E   W   E
S I E R R A   K R O N O R
```

7

```
  A L L I M P O R T A N T
I   O   D   L   O   M   E
N O V E L   I N S T A L L
G   A   E   G   E   S   E
R O B E   T H U M B S U P
A   L   S   T   A     R
T E E T E R   F R A N C O
I   N   I   Y   O   M
A D J U T A N T   S N I P
T   A   I   T   S   Z   T
I N C E N S E   N I E C E
N   O   E   N   U   R   R
G O B B L E D Y G O O K
```

8

```
T R A F F I C L I G H T S
W   M   A   L   S   I   T
E M U   C H A M P A G N E
R   S   T   M   Y   H   E
P R E C I O U S   S W A P
    M   O   P   A   A   E
T H E E N D   A B A T E D
W   N   S   P   U   E
I O T A   P O N D E R E D
N   P   R   P   H   M   O
S O A P O P E R A   A N T
E   R   O   Y   B   R   T
T A K E T H E M I C K E Y
```

9

10

11

12

SOLUTIONS

13

P	E	E	L		I	M	P	R	O	P	E	R
A		S				A		E		I		U
S	A	C	K		U	N	O	P	E	N	E	D
S		A		P		T		R		E		E
P	A	P	E	R	T	R	A	I	L			
O		A		O		A		M		R		L
R	E	D	U	C	E		P	A	C	I	N	O
T		E		L		S		N		D		P
			H	I	T	A	N	D	M	I	S	S
S		D		V		L		S		C		I
T	E	R	M	I	N	U	S		F	U	N	D
U		A		T		T				L		E
N	E	W	L	Y	W	E	D		H	E	E	D

14

	D	E	G	E	N	E	R	A	T	E		
	E		L		I		E		O		H	
C	L	E	A	N	C	U	T		T	R	O	T
	F		C		K		R		A		B	
T	W	I	G			T	E	L	L	I	N	G
		A		C		A					O	
R	U	L	E	O	F	T	H	U	M	B		
E				S		S		S		P		
P	A	S	T	I	M	E		E	D	I	T	
S		R		E		S		A		H		
S	O	D	A		T	I	P	S	T	E	R	S
N		I		I		E		E		O		
	B	L	A	C	K	W	I	D	O	W		

15

	P	E	R	P	E	T	U	A	T	E		
H	U		E		I		N		R			
O	U	T	C	A	S	T		B	L	U	R	B
T		O		L		H		E		S		A
B	U	N	G		P	E	D	A	N	T	I	C
L			F		R		T		E			K
O	R	A	C	L	E		D	E	M	E	A	N
O		F		O		F		N				U
D	A	F	F	O	D	I	L		W	H	A	M
E		L		D		A		C		U		B
D	R	I	L	L		S	P	L	U	R	G	E
		C		I		C		U		R		R
	S	T	A	T	I	O	N	E	R	Y		

16

D	R	A	M	A	T	I	C		P	A	S	S
I		C		P		N		H		N		P
S	T	R	A	P		D	R	E	D	G	E	R
H		O		R		U		A		L		I
	U	N	D	E	R	C	U	R	R	E	N	T
S		Y		C		E		T				Z
L	I	M	P	I	D		A	R	C	A	D	E
I			A	T		T		E		F		R
P	A	L	E	T	T	E	K	N	I	F	E	
S		O		I		R		D		A		D
H	O	W	E	V	E	R		I	M	B	U	E
O		E		E		O		N		L		N
D	I	R	T		F	R	A	G	M	E	N	T

17

```
T I D Y   O F F S H O O T
U   O   C   L   O   D   R
R E G A L I A   L O D G E
N   M   I   S   I   M   K
D R A W N   H I D D E N
O       I   I       N   A
W E L L C O N N E C T E D
N   E       T   F       H
  L A U N C H   F L U K E
B   R   O   E   A   N   S
R E N E W   P U C C I N I
E   E   A   A   E   O   V
W O R R Y I N G   O N C E
```

18

```
          F I G U R E O U T
S   E   L   O   I   R   R
C A N T O   B A B Y G R O
A   T   U   L   S   A   U
T H E O R I E S   S N U B
T   R   I   T   R   I   L
E X P O S E   T O U S L E
R   R   H   D   A   A   M
B R I M   V E N D E T T A
R   S   S   L   T   I   K
A N I M A T E   E V O K E
I   N   K   T   S   N   R
N E G L I G E N T
```

19

```
S U C K E R   P S Y C H E
I   A   L   P   Y   H   N
E E R I E   M E A D O W S
S   C   C   O   T   M   U
T O A S T E R   U P P E R
A   S   S   L       E
  S T A L E M A T E
S       I   C       X   G
L A T E R   O D D B A L L
A   A   F   D   E   C   A
P A S S A G E   F I T I N
U   T   R   E   L   C
P R E F E R   G R O Y N E
```

20

```
      F   D   H   T
  C U R R Y F A V O U R
  H   A   N   R   W   E
B E V Y   A R S O N I S T
E       M   H   H   P
D R A S T I C   B A T O N
L   E   C   G   L   N
M E A N S   A R T L E S S
A   T   F   E           I
A D D I T I O N   D E B T
E   E   N   A   R   L
R A N K A N D F I L E
      T   L   E   P
```

SOLUTIONS

21

22

23

24

25

```
  T H A N K S G I V I N G
B A   A   N   N   U
E U R O S   G R A N A R Y
A B   H   E   C   L   S
T R O Y   F L O T I L L A
T   U   W   Y   I   N
H A R R O W   E V E N E D
E     O   S   E   O   D
C L A D D I N G   O T T O
L   D   C   O   A   A   L
O R I N O C O   K A B U L
C   E   C   Z   I   L   S
K N U C K L E U N D E R
```

26

```
P I T C H E D B A T T L E
O   H   O   U   G   O   V
W O O   L O N G R A N G E
Y   R   L   C   A   G   R
S T O W A W A Y   J U D E
    U   N   N   B   E   S
P A G O D A   S A D I S T
E   H   E   V   C   N
L U G E   B A C K A C H E
I   O   D   C   L   H   V
C H I P O L A T A   E X E
A   N   M   N   S   E   N
N O G R E A T S H A K E S
```

27

```
S P I D E R M A N   C   V
  I   E   T   P O K E   R
U P P E R C U T S   L   R
  E   T   K   I   A L M S
C I   T O U C H   E   A
A L B I O N   A U F A I T
S   U   T     N   G   I
T I P P E T   A C T U A L
I   R   M A R S H   E   E
G O O D   U   S   P   C
A   F   I R R I T A B L E
T I E D   U   S   W   O
E   N   E S P I O N A G E
```

28

```
S O F A B E D   C   F   A
T   I   E   E G O T I S M
A C R Y L I C   N   E   U
S   E   I   A R T I S T S
H A D E S   M   R   T   E
  I     H A P H A Z A R D
  D   A   V     E
C A L I B R A T E     N
O   E   E   G   N A B O B
C O T T A G E   T   R   A
O   H   C   O R I G I N S
O N A R O L L   O   B   I
N   L   N   D U N G E O N
```

SOLUTIONS

29

30

31

32

33

```
. R O C K B O T T O M .
P . O . H . E . O . A .
R O W L I N G . P A R E D
O . D . P . O . N . S . A
S T Y X . U N C O M M O N
C . . . A . E . T . A . I
R E C O R D . S C E N T S
I . H . I . T . H . . H .
B L I Z Z A R D . D R U B
E . C . O . A . T . O . L
D R A I N . C A R I B O U
. . G . A . E . U . E . E
. T O W N C R I E R S . .
```

34

```
O D D B A L L S . S L I P
M . U . N . A . A . A . O
S I R E N . B O L S T E R
K . A . E . O . L . T . P
. A B S O L U T E Z E R O
S . L . F . R . M . . . I
T R E N C H . A B A T E S
O . . L . L . R . A . E .
P E R S E V E R A N C E .
O . O . V . G . C . T . I
V I S C E R A . I N F U N
E . E . S . T . N . U . C
R A S H . M O N G O L I A
```

35

```
C O A X . S C A B B A R D
H . D . B . O . R . L . I
A N D S O O N . I D L E R
P . E . S . C . E . E . K
L E D O N . E F F I G Y .
A . . . I . N . R . . A .
I N S T A N T A N E O U S
N . E . . . R . O . . S .
. R A F F I A . D U B A I
T . L . L . T . O . R . S
R A I S E . I N F R O N T
A . O . E . O . F . T . E
M O N O T O N E . S H E D
```

36

```
. . . M E L O D I O U S
H . B . O . I . O . N . W
A D O R N . G N O C C H I
L . R . O . H . R . E . N
F I D E L I T Y . K I N G
M . E . I . S . D . N . T
E R R A T A . P O T A S H
A . C . H . C . O . W . E
S L O W . T A J M A H A L
U . L . H . M . S . I . E
R E L E A S E . D E L T A
E . I . W . R . A . E . D
S P E A K E A S Y . . . .
```

SOLUTIONS

37

38

39

40

41

42

43

44

SOLUTIONS

45

	P	A	R	S	O	N	A	G	E		G		P
	D		U		E		A		C	O	V	E
F	A	I	R	Y	T	A	L	E		R		R
	M		F		T		L		J	E	E	P
J		I		S	L	O	O	P		V		L
A	U	N	T	I	E		P	L	A	I	C	E
M		S		N			A		D		X
P	U	T	P	U	T		F	I	N	A	L	E
A		I		S	H	O	O	T		L		D
C	A	T	S		R		R		S		G
K		U		C	U	B	B	Y	H	O	L	E
E	A	T	S		S		I		O		U
D		E		S	T	U	D	P	O	K	E	R

46

C	L	O	T	H	E	S		H		C		S
R		L		E		T	O	U	R	I	S	T
O	R	I	G	A	M	I		R		T		R
A		V		V		F	O	R	F	R	E	E
T	H	E	R	E		L		I		U		S
U			N	O	E	X	C	U	S	E	S
G		O			A			D
S	E	V	E	N	T	E	E	N		G
A		O		E		N		E	A	V	E	S
M	E	R	M	A	I	D		L		O		W
O		T		R		I	M	A	G	I	N	E
S	W	E	E	T	E	N		M		C		A
A		X		H		G	A	P	Y	E	A	R

47

	G	L	A	M	O	U	R	P	U	S	S	
F		I		A		M		E		M		S
U	N	T	E	N	A	B	L	E		A	G	O
N		T		R		V		R		L
A	B	H	O	R		I	C	E	D	T	E	A
N		O		A		A		C		R
D	R	O	O	P	Y		A	V	I	A	T	E
G		V		B		I		R		N
A	M	E	N	I	T	Y		N	U	D	G	E
M		R		M		L		T		R
E	N	D		P	L	A	I	N	S	O	N	G
S		A		E		W		E		L		Y
	S	M	A	L	L	S	C	R	E	E	N	

48

L	A	D	Y	O	F	T	H	E	L	A	K	E
	I		O		I		I		O		A
W	R	E	N		R	O	P	E	W	A	Y	S
	M		K		E		P		B		O
F	I	R	S	T	F	L	O	O	R		
	L			L		L			O		D
F	E	I	S	T	Y		H	O	W	Z	A	T
S		C				A				N
		H	U	R	D	Y	G	U	R	D	Y
F		E		E		R		N		R
D	I	S	R	A	E	L	I		C	R	U	X
N		Z		V		C		U		F
G	E	T	O	N	E	S	K	I	T	O	F	F

49

50

51

52

SOLUTIONS

53

```
B A L M _ C H E R U B I C
A _ U _ E _ I _ E _ R
B U G B E A R _ P I Q U E
Y _ E _ L _ T _ E _ U _ W
B A S I C _ F U N N E L _
O _ _ R _ O _ _ _ S _ P
O U T B O A R D M O T O R
M _ I _ _ D _ U _ _ _ I
_ S N A C K S _ D I G I N
O _ F _ H _ H _ D _ A _ T
P R O M O _ I N L I M B O
U _ I _ I _ R _ E _ M _ U
S A L A R I E D _ R A F T
```

54

```
_ _ _ C O R K S C R E W
O _ I _ R _ E _ I _ H _ H
V E N U E _ B A Z O O K A
E _ T _ A _ O _ E _ D _ T
R E E F K N O T _ B O N E
N _ R _ I _ T _ S _ D _ V
I M M U N E _ C O H E R E
G _ E _ G _ E _ L _ N _ R
H I D E _ E M B O L D E N
T _ I _ A _ B _ I _ R _ E
B R A V U R A _ S I O U X
A _ R _ R _ R _ T _ N _ T
G U Y F A W K E S _ _ _ _
```

55

```
B I C E P S _ S H A D O W
L _ H _ R _ _ A _ A _ R
O R A T E _ N O M I N E E
B _ M _ S _ U _ S _ D _ A
B L O S S O M _ T R Y S T
Y _ I _ _ B _ E _ _ _ H
_ _ S C A R E C R O W _ _
C _ _ T _ R _ _ _ H _ S
A R A B S _ O B E L I S K
N _ L _ T _ N _ M _ P _ E
C O I N A G E _ P A P A W
E _ E _ K _ _ T _ E _ E
R E N D E R _ O Y S T E R
```

56

```
_ _ B _ P _ A _ I _ _
_ S Q U A R E D A N C E _
H _ N _ O _ O _ V _ J
N E C K _ T H R E A T E N
L _ _ E _ N _ S _ C
G O O D E G G _ V I S T A
_ V _ I _ E _ C _ O _ O
D E F O E _ L A U N D R Y
_ S _ C _ C _ Y _ _ S
B Y G E O R G E _ F E E T
_ O _ S _ O _ N _ A _ A
U P A G A I N S T I T
_ _ N _ K _ E _ E _ _
```

57

```
  K   L   A   A
  O X O F F I C E
D   H   C   F   E   U
S O U L   U P R I S I N G
Y   R   S   A       D
C O B A L T   Y I P P E E
U   B       L   R
I M P I S H   F L U F F Y
I       U   U   M   I
I N S T I N C T   B A R K
D   O   G   U   I   E
  M I R R O R I N G
  L   Y   E   G
```

58

```
C O M M U T E R T R A I N
O   A   L X   A   D   O
B Y R O N I C   M A D A M
    Q   A   I   A   L   I
C L U B   S T U R G E O N
A   I   G   E   I   A
R E S U L T   U N B O L T
B   O   B   D   V   E
U N T O W A R D   H E R D
N   A   W   A   B   R
C A R G O   C O L L A G E
L   S   R   E   O   R   V
E R I C M O R E C A M B E
```

59

```
  R A B B I T   S W I S H
  A   R   R   U   N   O
D I W A L I   U N E V E N
L   C   S   N   A   E
J I V E   H I B I S C U S
N   R   S   E   U   T
  G L O T T A L S T O P
U U   E   L   A   E
M I L K Y W A Y   P O P E
L L   E   F   R   P
A R A R A T   L O O T E R
U B   R   O   O   R
T R Y O N   A P A T H Y
```

60

```
D O O D L E   C O M B A T
E   W E   B   F   L   U
P A N A C E A   F L O U R
I   E   T   C   E   W   R
C U R V E   K A R A O K E
T   R   T   U   T
  D O W N T O E A R T H
T U   F   C   J
O U T D O O R   C H I N A
U   C   D   O   U   N
C L O U D   N E S T E G G
H   M   L T   E   R   L
E V E L Y N   W R I T H E
```

SOLUTIONS

61

62

63

64

65

66

67

68

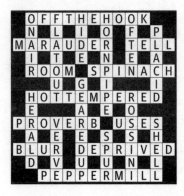

SOLUTIONS

69

70

71

72

73

```
S U P P L Y . M A D C A P
E . Y . A . . D . R . . R
E N J O Y . A R A P A H O
T . A . E . U . M . Z . N
H U M E R U S . A G E N T
E . A . T . N . . . . . O
. S U P E R S T A R . . .
S . H . I . . . . I . . G
P A T I O . A B A L O N E
I . I . N . M . T . . . O
R E P R E S S . P R O U D
I . S . I . . . L . U . E
T R Y I N G . C E N S U S
```

74

```
. . F . S . F . F . . . .
J O I N T H E C L U B . .
U . L . A . R . E . O . .
O G R E . C O N V E R G E
G . . K . S . T . . S . .
B E A C H E D . B I T T Y
R . A . D . G . N . A . .
S N O U T . B R I G A N D
A . S . T . E . . . D . .
L U K E W A R M . G E A R
T . W . M . L . U . R . .
S H A R P W I T T E D . .
. Y . A . N . S . . . . .
```

75

```
. . D . T . R . F . . . .
. B O U R G E O I S . . .
V . W . I . W . S . I . .
M I E N . F R A C T U R E
C . P . L . R . . . R . .
R E M O T E . D I P P E R
V . U . . . . . I . G . .
B E A R U P . F U N R U N
R . . A . A . P . L . . .
E S O T E R I C . R O A M
A . O . I . T . I . R . .
. S O F T T O U C H . . .
. T . Y . R . K . . . . .
```

76

```
T R A N Q U I L L I S E R
O . N . U . N . U . H . E
M I D R I F F . S P O O F
. . R O D . O . C . R . E
P L O T . A R T I S T I C
A . I . T . M . O . . . T
P O D I U M . G U N G H O
E . . . R . S . S . R . R
R E C E N T L Y . W A V Y
B . R . B . I . B A N . .
A R E N A . P L U N D E R
C . D . C . O . . E . U .
K N O C K O N E F F E C T
```

SOLUTIONS

77

78

79

80

81

```
L A U D A T O R Y . R . D
. H . E . R . U . D E A R
M O R E C A M B E . C . O
. Y . P . V . B . S T E M
A . S . B E L L Y . A . E
F I T F U L . E A R N E D
O . E . I . . . R . G . A
R E V O L T . A N T L E R
E . E . T I T U S . E . Y
H I N D . N . B . E . S .
A . S . S K Y R O C K E T
N O O N . E . E . H . E .
D . N . G R E Y H O U N D
```

82

```
R E B U F F S . S . M . L
O . R . L . A C H I E V E
P E A F O W L . O . D . S
E . K . A . A S U S U A L
S P E N T . A . L . S . I
. A . I M M E D I A T E .
. I . N . . . E . . A .
S L A U G H T E R . . L .
H . U . V . I . B L O K E
I N G R O U P . L . U . R
F . U . T . T R A I N E E
T O R P E D O . D . C . C
Y . Y . R . P R E S E N T
```

83

```
. B A C K S L I D I N G .
H . C . I . O . W . U . M
A T T E N T I V E . L E A
N . . D . T . L . L . . R
D E T E R . E C L A I R S
T E E . R . . . F . . H .
O V E R D O . A F F I R M
M . N . . B . U . E . . A
O T A L G I A . N O D A L
U . G . A . R . G . . . L
T I E . M A R C O P O L O
H . R . B . E . U . N . W
. E S T A B L I S H E D .
```

84

```
A C C O M M O D A T I O N
. A . R . Y . E . R . N .
G R A B . . S T I L E T T O
. D . I . T . G . A . O .
H I S T R I O N I C . . .
. G . . . F . . . L . F .
B A R L E Y . S E E M L Y
. N . E . . . T . . . O .
. . . B I L L E T D O U X
. H . A . O . A . E . N .
T O W N H A L L . M O D E
. U . O . D . T . O . E .
F R A N Z S C H U B E R T
```

SOLUTIONS

85

86

87

88

89

```
G A M E ▪ S O M E R S E T
A A Z Y ▪ L A ▪ I
D R Y N E S S ▪ E X P E L
A O A T C I E
B E R Y L ▪ E S T E E M ▪
O ▪ O R ▪ N O
U N A N T I C I P A T E D
T T A A Y
▪ S T R A I T ▪ L E A K S
E R L C A D S
P I A N O ▪ H E C T A R E
I C N E E G U
C A T E G O R Y ▪ M E S S
```

90

```
▪ ▪ A S C E R T A I N
I G S A O R O
N E A R S S O L D I E R
C I E I E S T
O I N T M E N T ▪ U T A H
M S B O H O E
P E B B L E ▪ C O P P E R
A O E C L H N
R A R E ▪ P L A Y B A L L
A O C A R N I
B L U S H E R ▪ O C E A N
L G U E O S E
E X H I B I T E D ▪ ▪
```

91

```
L I B I D O ▪ S C A T T Y
A R W A I A
V O I C E H A N D G U N
I G L Y T E K
S T A R T E D A G R E E
H D E T D
▪ E X C O R I A T E ▪
S O A T U
C H A S M B A C C H U S
A U P A E I E
R E D W O O D L U C I D
E I S L A U
D U T I E S ▪ R O L L U P
```

92

```
▪ T A ▪ S D ▪
M A R Y P O P P I N S
A I P U S A
F L O P A I R C R A F T
E R N A E
A D M I R E R D E A T H
I R L B L Y
O C H R E S A T I S F Y
T I T L I
V I C T O R I A P O R E
O A I N A S
N O N D E S C R I P T
▪ T S E N ▪
```

SOLUTIONS

93

94

95

96

```
  S O U T H A F R I C A N
C   B   E   N   E   Y   O
H O V E R   C A V E M A N
I   I   M   H   I   R   S
E L A N   S O Y S A U C E
F   T   C   R   I       Q
O R E G O N   H O N S H U
F     S   R   N   K   I
S T R I M M E R   E Y O T
T   I   E   C   S   L   U
A P O S T L E   C H A I R
F   J   I   S   A   R   S
F R A N C I S D R A K E
```

```
H A N D B R A K E T U R N
O   O   I   C   T   S   A
T I T   R A C O N T E U R
E   M   D   R   A   R   R
L A Y A B O U T   P I S A
    C   A   E   B   N   T
J A U N T Y   C U P T I E
O   P   H   M   L   E
G O O F   C O C K E R E L
T   F   B   N   H   F   O
R A T I O N A L E   A C T
O   E   O   C   A   C   U
T H A N K G O O D N E S S
```

```
C O S M O L O G Y   D   B
  I   E   O   U   V I S A
I I N T E N S I F Y   V   R
  K   K   E   F   J E E R
C   P   L I L A C   R   O
H E R M I T   W A R S A W
I   E   T     B   I   B
R U C K U S   B I S T R O
O   I   P Y L O N   Y   Y
P O S Y   N   A   I   B
O   E   S T A T U T O R Y
D O L E   A   E   E   U
Y   Y   E X T R E M I T Y
```

```
C H A S S I S   G   U   B
O   C   P   T R O U N C E
S E T F A I R   O   C   D
T   U   C   A R D U O U S
A P P L E   F   Q   R   I
  A     I C E B U C K E T
  R   N     E       A
F R E E V E R S E     S
A   N   A   O   N A V E L
J A C K D A W   B   O   I
I   A   E   I T E M I S E
T A M A R I N   S   L   I
A   P   S   G A S M A I N
```

SOLUTIONS

101

102

103

104

105

```
  P A L M S U N D A Y
W   I   E   P   E   D
H O G W A S H   C A M U S
I   I   D   I   K   I   U
T A T I   S N O W D R O P
E     F   X   E   A     E
D A M S O N   M A H L E R
W   A   R   E   R       D
A C R I M O N Y   B A K U
R   A   L   A   T   D   P
F A B L E   M A Y P O L E
    O   S   E   P   L   R
  D U S S E L D O R F
```

106

```
T A K E C A R E   P R O F
R   O   O   O   C   A   U
A L B U M   C L A R I O N
Y   L   E   O   R   T   C
  R E C A L C I T R A N T
S   N   C   O   O       I
L I Z A R D   M O J I T O
A       O   G   N   C   N
P O P U P T O A S T E R
D   I   P   A   T   O   S
A N C I E N T   R A V E L
S   T   R   E   I   E   A
H A S H   J E O P A R D Y
```

107

```
D U D E   E G G T I M E R
O   O   S   R   H   I   U
L O Z E N G E   R I L E D
D   E   A   E   O   L   E
R U N U P   K U W A I T
U     U   A       O     C
M O N O P O L Y M O N E Y
S   O       P   U       C
  S T I T C H   F O C A L
S   H   O   A   F   R   A
H O I C K   B E L G I U M
I   N   E   E   E   M   E
P A G I N A T E   W E A N
```

108

```
    C R E A M H O R N
E   A   H   M   O   N   A
M A L T A   B L O T T E R
A   I   N   R   D   H   R
N A K E D E Y E   N E M O
C   E   L   O   C   H   W
I N L I E U   R E F O R M
P   Y   R   K   L   R   I
A L S O   C I V I L I A N
T   T   M   T   B   Z   D
O D O R O U S   A R O S E
R   R   D   C   C   N   D
S T Y L I S H L Y
```

SOLUTIONS

109

110

111

112

113

```
. N E V A D A . . C H A M P
. E . A . E . . I . R . . S
A T O N A L . A R C A N A .
W . U . U . . . C . B . . L
N O V A . . T I T A N I U M
R . T . E . W . . C . . . S
. K N U C K L E H E A D . .
S . I . E . N . . N . . E .
C A T A L Y S T . . G O A D
H . P . I . . Y . . R . N .
O R I E N T . . T R A V E L
O . C . E . . . W . V . R .
L I K E N . C O M E L Y . .
```

114

```
J O S T L E . P U R S U E .
A . T . U . C . T . O . . S
C A R A M E L . U N L I T .
K . U . B . O . R . V . . A
E X T R A . C O N T E N T .
T . . . G . K . . . N . . E
. U N F O R T U N A T E . .
A . O . . . O . . O . . . P
D I S A V O W . U M B E R .
O . E . A . E . R . R . . I
R E G A L . R U I N O U S .
E . A . U . S . S . O . . S
D A Y B E D . S H O D D Y .
```

115

```
. I L L C O N C E I V E D
D . E . U . E . M . I . R
E R O D E . S P I N D L E
S . T . S . T . G . E . S
S H A M . G L O R I O U S
E . R . R . E . A . . . I
R E D E E M . S T R A I N
T . . . A . R . E . M . G
S I D E S T E P . F A I R
P . R . S . M . R . L . O
O V E R U S E . A G G R O
O . A . R . D . S . A . M
N U R S E R Y R H Y M E .
```

116

```
B U T T E R F I N G E R S
A . R . N . O . O . N . W
S P A . M O U S T A C H E
I . N . E . L . E . O . E
C A S T S O U T . R U S T
. . M . H . P . O . R . I
B O I L E R . I M P A L E
A . G . D . I . N . G . .
T U R N . I N D I R E C T
C . A . L . F . V . M . E
H O T P O T A T O . E R R
E . O . R . N . R . N . S
S T R E E T T H E A T R E
```

SOLUTIONS

117

118

119

120

121

G	O	S	H			Q	U	E	E	N	B	E	E
A		C				N		N		O			D
N	E	A	T			P	R	E	T	E	N	C	E
G		N		S		U		H		D			N
R	I	D	I	C	U	L	O	U	S				
E		I		R		Y		S		M			B
N	E	U	T	E	R		G	I	G	O	L	O	
E		M		E		L		A		N			D
		U	N	D	E	R	S	T	U	D	Y		
G		O		T		G		T		M			B
R	E	V	I	E	W	E	R		W	E	L	L	
E		A		S		N			N				O
W	E	L	L	T	O	D	O		S	T	E	W	

122

N	E	A	R	M	I	S	S	E	S				
	E		B		O		Y		A		U		
H	E	I	R	L	O	O	M		S	I	N	K	
	D		I		N		P		E		D		
S	I	D	E			F	A	L	L	G	U	Y	
			G			E		T			L		
P	I	E	I	N	T	H	E	S	K	Y			
R			L			Y		T					
D	I	A	G	R	A	M			C	R	O	W	
M		A		R		T		U		O			
B	E	E	F			G	R	A	N	D	E	U	R
D		F		E		N		E		N			
	B	E	D	R	A	G	G	L	E	D			

123

		A	U	D	I	T	O	R	I	U	M		
W		S		R		H		O		N			
E	P	I	C	U	R	E		M	O	P	U	P	
A		D		M		S		A		A		I	
K	E	E	P		P	I	N	N	A	C	L	E	
W			K		S		T		K			D	
I	N	T	E	N	T		M	I	A	S	M	A	
L		I		I		P		C				T	
L	O	C	A	T	I	O	N		T	W	E	E	
E		K		W		I		F		I		R	
D	R	O	N	E		S	H	E	L	T	E	R	
	F		A		O		T		T			E	
	E	F	F	R	O	N	T	E	R	Y			

124

S	U	S	P	E	N	S	E		A	G	U	E	
A		L		M		H		R		N			
S	C	E	N	E		E	L	E	M	E	N	T	
H		P		V		L		N		T		R	
	S	T	E	E	P	L	E	C	H	A	S	E	
O		I		N		Y		E				A	
F	I	N	I	T	E		A	F	F	E	C	T	
F			H		F		O		M			Y	
W	E	A	T	H	E	R	P	R	O	O	F		
H		C		O		E		W		T		F	
I	N	T	R	U	D	E		A	L	I	V	E	
T		O		R		Z		R		V		E	
E	A	R	N		H	E	A	D	R	E	S	T	

SOLUTIONS

125

A	G	E	S		W	R	O	N	G	F	U	L
P		A		W		O		I		O		E
P	A	R	V	E	N	U		G	O	R	S	E
R		T		I		N		H		M		S
O	T	H	E	R		D	E	T	A	I	L	
A			D		T				C		D	
C	U	T	T	O	T	H	E	C	H	A	S	E
H		R			E		H		C			
	T	A	C	T	I	C		U	S	A	G	E
P		I		I		L		M		S		A
O	U	T	R	E		O	S	M	O	S	I	S
R		O		U		C		Y		E		E
T	U	R	N	P	I	K	E		S	T	U	D

126

			C	O	U	R	T	S	H	I	P
L		B		R		N		O		I		A
E	L	U	D	E		I	N	S	U	R	E	R
A		R		D		T		S		E		A
D	O	G	T	I	R	E	D		S	P	U	D
I		L		B		D		M		U		E
N	E	A	R	L	Y		O	I	L	R	I	G
G		R		E		Z		L		C		R
L	O	A	D		B	A	L	L	Y	H	O	O
I		L		O		G		R		A		U
G	R	A	M	M	A	R		A	R	S	O	N
H		R		I		E		C		E		D
T	I	M	E	T	A	B	L	E			

127

B	E	C	O	M	E		I	M	P	A	I	R
A		L		O			Y		L			E
N	A	I	A	D		P	A	S	S	I	V	E
I		M		E		O		T		A		K
S	W	A	L	L	O	W		I	S	S	U	E
H		T			D		F					D
		E	A	G	L	E	E	Y	E	D		
T			A		R		I			I		S
W	A	L	T	Z		K	I	N	G	P	I	N
O		O		E		E		A		L		I
B	A	C	K	L	O	G		C	L	O	U	T
I		A		L		R		M		M		C
T	E	L	L	E	R		D	E	T	A	C	H

128

		S		T		S		I			
	P	A	C	K	E	D	L	U	N	C	H
	A		A		A		O		S		A
S	N	O	B		C	U	P	B	O	A	R	D
I			O		S		L		U		
E	C	S	T	A	S	Y		S	E	A	M	Y
B		O		Y		G		N		S	
B	U	R	L	Y		P	O	R	T	I	C	O
T		E		M		A		A			A
S	T	A	R	F	I	S	H		T	O	R	N
O		A		N		E		O		U	
N	A	T	I	O	N	A	L	I	S	M	
		E		R		D		L			

129

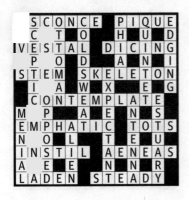

130

131

132

133

```
  V E N U S F L Y T R A P
C . M . R . O . I . O . R
A S P E N . E X E C U T E
T . R . S . T . L . S . P
A M E N . S A N D I E G O
S . S . Q . L . I . . . S
T I S S U E . I N M O S T
R . . . A . V . G . R . E
O V E R D R A W . A G A R
P . A . R . N . A . A . O
H A R V A R D . B A N T U
I . L . N . A . E . Z . S
C R Y S T A L C L E A R .
```

134

```
P U S I L L A N I M O U S
U . O . O . F . V . L . H
T O O . P U F F A D D E R
U . N . S . O . N . W . I
P R E M I E R E . K I E V
. . R . D . D . M . V . E
P R O P E R . C E R E A L
I . R . D . E . L . S . .
B U L K . E L E V A T O R
R . A . B . P . I . A . I
O N T H E B A L L . L I P
C . E . L . S . L . E . O
H O R A T I O N E L S O N
```

135

```
B R E A K F A S T . G . P
. A . C . I . I . L A D Y
I A P H R O D I T E . R . O
. T . E . G . T . K I L N
P . A . L E V E L . B . G
R E P E A T . R O M A N Y
O . P . K . . . U . L . A
P L A N E T . W I S D E N
A . L . S H O E S . I . G
G O L F . U . A . S . A .
A . I . B R I L L I A N T
T A N K . S . T . G . N .
E . G . C O C H I N E A L
```

136

```
T I R A D E S . C . M . D
A . U . I . H I R S U T E
C O L O G N E . E . T . B
I . E . F . A M M E T E R
T O R S O . R . E . O . I
. P . . . R E S I D E N T S
. A . . V . . . E . . . O
A L U M I N I U M . . . W
I . N . C . N . E B O N Y
R A T A T A T . N . M . O
B . I . O . O N T R A C K
A N D I R O N . H . H . E
G . Y . Y . E Y E B A L L
```

137

```
. P A R T I C I P A T E .
W . R . O . H . A . A . G
A T T O R N E Y S . R U E
R . . M . E . T . A . N .
T O Q U E . S T A I N E D
S . U . N . E . . T . A .
A D A P T S . H A Z I E R
N . S . . M . N . N . M .
D R I P D R Y . A T O N E
A . M . E . O . G . . R .
L E O . P A P A R A Z Z I
L . D . O . I . A . E . E
. F O R T H C O M I N G .
```

138

```
P A Y A N D D I S P L A Y
. C . O . E . R . A . U .
S T A R . C O A S T I N G
. I . T . R . T . E . T .
A N N A S E W E L L . . .
. I . . E . . L . . L . .
R U M P U S . T R A G I C
. M . O . . . R . . M . .
. . R E C T A N G L E S .
. J . T . H . C . O . R .
P U G I L I S T . F A I L
. D . O . E . O . E . C .
G O I N G F O R B R O K E
```

139

```
H E E L . D I S P U T E S
E . I . . N . E . Y . U .
P I N E . I N T R E P I D
T . S . P . A . I . E . S
A L T E R A T I O N . . .
G . E . O . E . D . F . N
O P I A T E . M I L I E U
N . N . R . H . C . R . I
. . C A R E T A K E R S .
G . K . C . R . L . W . A
R I N G T O N E . Y A R N
O . O . E . I . . L . C .
W I T H D R A W . B L U E
```

140

```
. F I G U R E H E A D . .
. I . L . I . E . G . A .
I N F A M O U S . I M P S
. A . D . T . I . N . P .
. L I D O . S T A G G E R
. . E . G . A . . . A . .
C O N J E C T U R A L . .
O . . R . E . U . . . . .
P R O M I S E . P L U G .
S . I . H . E . E . L . .
C E N T . W A L K O V E R
T . R . I . L . U . A . .
. D E A N M A R T I N . .
```

SOLUTIONS

141

142

143

144

145

146

147

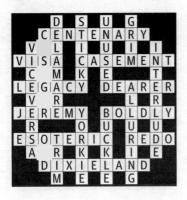

148

SOLUTIONS

149

	A	P	A	T	H	Y		K	U	D	O	S
		T		B		I		O		A		A
L	A	P	D	O	G		C	A	S	U	A	L
	N		O		H		L		P			O
R	E	A	M		S	E	R	A	P	H	I	M
	N		E		P		E		I		E	
	D	U	N	F	E	R	M	L	I	N	E	
A		N		E		I		N		N		
B	E	H	O	L	D	E	N		C	A	D	S
R		A		I		I		L		L		U
U	P	P	I	T	Y		S	Q	U	I	R	M
P		P		H		C		D		E		
T	H	Y	M	E		B	E	H	E	A	D	

150

L	O	V	A	G	E		T	A	R	Z	A	N
O		A		R		C		R		I		I
V	O	L	C	A	N	O		G	U	L	A	G
E		I		N		N		O		L		G
R	A	D	I	I		S	U	N	D	I	A	L
S				T		I				O		E
	E	F	F	A	N	D	B	L	I	N	D	
O		A		E		A						L
W	H	I	S	K	E	R		C	O	C	O	A
N		L		A		A		O		H		N
S	K	I	M	P		T	A	N	K	A	R	D
U		N		U		E		I		F		E
P	I	G	S	T	Y		S	C	R	E	E	D

151

	S	P	I	R	I	T	U	A	L	I	T	Y
A		O		A		I		V		N		E
L	A	S	E	R		P	R	I	M	U	L	A
P		T		E		P		A		R		S
H	O	W	L		V	E	S	T	M	E	N	T
A		A		F		D		I				E
B	O	R	Z	O	I		C	O	C	C	Y	X
E				R		Q		N		H		T
T	H	A	N	K	F	U	L		D	E	A	R
S		G		L		I		J		A		A
O	V	A	T	I	O	N		A	Z	T	E	C
U		I		F		C		C		O		T
P	O	N	Y	T	R	E	K	K	I	N	G	

152

B	U	S	H	T	E	L	E	G	R	A	P	H
U		U		H		A		I		R		Y
I	N	N		U	N	D	E	R	P	A	I	D
L		W		R		D		O		B		R
T	O	O	L	S	H	E	D		L	I	M	A
		R		D		R		B		C		N
B	I	S	C	A	Y		P	U	N	N	E	T
L		H		Y		R		L		U		
U	K	I	P		B	E	R	G	A	M	O	T
E		P		F		S		A		E		R
T	A	P	D	A	N	C	E	R		R	Y	E
I		E		S		U		I		A		S
T	U	R	N	T	H	E	T	A	B	L	E	S

153

```
T A L K A T I V E   V   O
  J H   I   O   K I E V
I S A L A D D A Y S   C   E
  R   N   D   E   V E I N
A   I   C L O U T   S   R
P U N C H Y   R I S Q U E
P   S   A   G   U   A
A C I D I C   H E R A L D
L   D   R O T O R   D   Y
L A I D   N   M   S   A
I   O   A D V A N T A G E
N O U N   O   G   A   O
G   S   G R E E N G A G E
```

154

```
I N A S T E W   A   E   A
N   M   A   I N C I T E D
T H I C K E N   Q   H   A
E   S   E   T O U R I N G
R E S A T   R   I   C   I
  V       H E Y P R E S T O
  I   E       E       H
F L U M M O X E D   A
O   P   I   A   T O P I C
S I L I C O N   A   I   R
S   I   K   A B S O L V E
I N F I E L D   T   A   E
L   T   Y   U N E Q U A L
```

155

```
  C A R D I O G R A P H
S   L   O   P   E   U   C
H O L Y G R A I L   B U Y
O   S   Q   I   L   B
R E S E T   U N T W I N E
T   I   A   E   S   R
L U X U R Y   A F G H A N
I   T   W   A   E   E
S C H O L A R   T A R O T
T   F   I   I   I   I
E G O   C A T E G O R I C
D   R   I   H   U   A   S
  S M I T H E R E E N S
```

156

```
G A L L O W S H U M O U R
  N O   A   E   O   K
T A L C   S P R O C K E T
  T   U   S   T   K   S
C H I M P A N Z E E
E   I       R   S
A M O R A L   C O Y O T E
  A   E       Y       I
    C A T S C R A D L E
E   I   E   L   N   E
O R A T O R I O   T U T U
  G   E   M   N   I   T
C O N D E S C E N S I O N
```

SOLUTIONS

157

158

159

160

161

```
R A P E   O F F S T A G E
U   R S U     A   I     X
B R O W N I E   N O R M A
B   N   A   L   T   P   M
I N G O T     I C A R U S
S     C     N     M     S
H I T T H E J A C K P O T
Y   H     E     O       R
  P E L V I C   H A I T I
A   L     I   T   O   D K
F E I G N   I S R A E L I
A   K   Y   Y O T   A   N
R I E S L I N G   S L O G
```

162

```
      A S P A R A G U S
O D   S   I   U   R   T
U M A M I   C A N T O N A
T   I   T   K   G   U   G
W E R E W O L F   E P E E
A   Y   E   E   W   C   W
R E P O R T   P O T A S H
D   R   E   A   R   P   I
B U O Y   C L E M A T I S
O   D   Z   A   H   A   P
U S U R E R S   O L I V E
N   C   U   K   L   N   R
D E E P S P A C E
```

163

```
D E J A V U   W A Y O U T
E   U   O     Q   T     R
F U S E D   D O U G H T Y
E   T   K   O   A   E   I
C E N T A V O   R E R U N
T   O       N   I       G
    W A S T E L A N D
J       M   S       I   I
A L P H A   B I O M A S S
B   L   C   I   O   B   A
B L A N K E T   M A O R I
E   N   E   P   L   A
D R E A R Y   W H O O S H
```

164

```
    E   S   S   W
M U D S L I N G I N G
E   G   O   E   C   U
B R A Y   B R E A K I N G
I       B   R   E   C
S T I F F E N   E D G A R
O   O   R   P   L   R
A C T O R   G R U Y E R E
R   T   E   O       I
C A T F I G H T   W R A P
C   A   G   E   O   G
Y E L L O W S T O N E
    L   N   T   F
```

SOLUTIONS

165

166

167

168

169

	S	E	L	F	A	B	S	O	R	B	E	D
P	X	A		O	N		R		E
O	C	C	U	R		N	E	T	B	A	L	L
I	L	E		E	N	H		V		I
N	O	U	S		T	I	M	E	B	O	M	B
T	D	S		E	D		E		E
S	C	E	N	I	C		B	O	T	H	E	R
O			X	K	T	E	A
F	I	R	S	T	A	I	D		G	R	I	T
V	A	I	S	A	C	E
I	N	G	R	E	S	S		S	K	U	L	L
E	G	T	E	I	L	Y
W	E	A	T	H	E	R	V	A	N	E	S	

170

A	D	M	I	N	I	S	T	R	A	T	O	R
M	I	E	A	A	O	O
B	U	S	G	I	V	E	I	T	A	G	O
E	U	A	A	N	D	K
R	I	N	G	T	O	N	E	F	I	N	E
D	I	T	P	N	R
S	L	E	E	V	E	G	R	O	T	T	Y
A	R	E	R	I	H
V	A	S	E	W	I	T	C	H	E	R	Y
A	T	R	G	E	H	I
G	R	A	P	E	S	H	O	T	O	A	K
E	N	L	T	A	L	E
D	A	D	D	Y	L	O	N	G	L	E	G	S

171

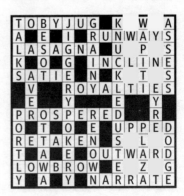

S	C	R	E	W	B	A	L	L	B	S
U	M	U	I	R	E	S	T
A	R	B	I	T	R	A	T	E	T	A
B	T	D	M	C	R	A	M
S	E	S	E	R	U	M	O	P
O	R	D	A	I	N	S	A	L	T	E	D
T	I	N	D	H	U
T	U	T	T	U	T	O	L	D	E	S	T
O	O	S	E	E	D	Y	D	Y
V	E	R	Y	A	D	D	B
O	I	A	M	B	I	G	U	O	U	S
C	R	A	G	U	T	M	G
E	L	U	P	S	Y	D	A	I	S	Y

172

T	O	B	Y	J	U	G	K	W	A
A	E	I	R	U	N	W	A	Y	S
L	A	S	A	G	N	A	U	P	S
K	O	G	I	N	C	L	I	N	E
S	A	T	I	E	N	K	T	S
V	R	O	Y	A	L	T	I	E	S
E	Y	E	Y
P	R	O	S	P	E	R	E	D	R
O	T	O	E	U	P	P	E	D
R	E	T	A	K	E	N	S	L	O
T	A	E	O	U	T	W	A	R	D
L	O	W	B	R	O	W	E	Z	G
Y	A	Y	N	A	R	R	A	T	E

SOLUTIONS

173

174

175

176

177

```
  P I A N I S S I M O
W   A   L   N   A   O
R A N K L E S   L U C I D
I   E   Y   A   U   K   E
S I L T   I N S T I N C T
T       B   E   A   E   E
W I C K E R   P R A Y E R
A   H   D   O   Y       M
T H A L L I U M   R O T I
C   R   I   T   C   W   N
H U M A N   C A Y E N N E
    E   E   R   A   U   D
  B R A N D Y S N A P
```

178

```
H A R M L E S S   F L I P
I   E   E   U   C   E   L
C O P I T   P R O R A T A
K   R   T   P   N   R   C
  L I F E S E N T E N C E
E   N   R   R   E       N
M O T I O N   I M P A C T
P       P   C   P   R   A
H A U T E C O U T U R E
A   L   N   D   U   A   A
S U C C E E D   O P I U M
I   E   R   L   U   G   I
S A R S   R E A S O N E D
```

179

```
B O L D   A M I C A B L E
Y   A   B   U   A   A   M
C U R I O U S   B E S O M
H   G   N   I   I   M   Y
A B E A M   C O N F A B
N       O   A   T       S
C O N S T E L L A T I O N
E   U       C   V       I
  C R O T C H   E A T U P
A   S   E   A   N   I   P
P R I S M   I N G E N U E
E   N   P   R   E   G   T
D O G H O U S E   V E T S
```

180

```
        I M P R E S S E D
M   M   D   U   D   L   I
A B I D E   L E G L E S S
T   S   N   L   E   E   I
T U R N T A I L   S P I N
E   E   I   N   D   W   T
R E P U T E   B E H A V E
O   R   Y   A   P   L   G
F L E X   O N L O O K E R
F   S   K   G   R   I   A
A C E T O N E   T E N E T
C   N   H   L   E   G   E
T I T I L L A T E
```

SOLUTIONS

181

```
T R E N C H   C R U S T S
R   M   A       I   P   I
A M B E R   M I S L E A D
U   A   O   O   O   N   I
M O R E L L O   T I T A N
A   G     N   T         G
  O V E R S H O O T
A     C   H       E   C
S E T T O   I N C I S O R
Y   I   L   N   A   T   A
L U G H O L E   B R I E F
U   E   G     E   N   T
M A R T Y R   G R O G G Y
```

182

```
    S   A   S   E
  C O N T R E T E M P S
  O   A   R   A   U U
S M O G   E N V E L O P E
  P       A   E   S   E
C O M P E R E   M I T R E
  S   R   S   P   O   I
A T S E A   P E T N A M E
  H   S   T   A       P
T E A S P O O N   B O O K
  A   U   N   U   O   S
  P E R S I S T E N C E
    E   C   S   Y
```

183

```
    S   A   A   H
  S T A G E D O O R
  F   A   E D O   F
W O N T   N A I L F I L E
  L   U   T   C     O
  A L L A Y S   T A L L O W
  O   R       A     R
S W A Y E D   C L U M P S
  I   U   R   G   L
I N E D I B L E   H O A R
  G   O   L   C   T   N
    E N L I G H T E N
    E   N   E   R
```

184

```
I N E X P R E S S I B L E
N   N   E   N   P   I X
S U R F E I T   A N J O U
    O   R   I   R   O   B
M A U L   S C H E D U L E
I   T   B   E   R       R
S T E E L Y   R I V E R A
G     U   U   B   X   N
I N C I D E N T   P O R T
V   H   G   E   T   T
I N A N E   V I E W I N G
N   N   O   E   C   C E
G E T I N O N T H E A C T
```

185

```
  P A R O D Y   C A R V E
  R   E   I   A   A   L
M E R G E R   S V E L T E
  M   U   E   I   L   V
H I L L   C O A L M I N E
  U   A   T   V   E   N
  M A R G I N A L I S E
P   R   V   L   M   C
E T C E T E R A   M O O T
N   H   R   N   O   N
T R I P O D   C O R D O N
U   V   P   H   A   M
P I E C E   M E D L E Y
```

186

```
M U N I C H   S P I C E S
U   I   H   S   U   O   T
T E Q U I L A   T U D O R
A   A   M   N   O   E   A
T A B L E   C O N V I C T
E       R   H       N   A
  G I L A M O N S T E R
S   M       P   E       F
T E M P U R A   T U T O R
I   E   S   N   B   H   I
C A N O E   Z E A L O U S
K   S   U   A   C   R   K
S L E E P Y   S K I N N Y
```

187

```
  M O N E Y S P I N N E R
C   C   R   O   N   O   I
R A T E S   R E F U T E D
A   U   E   T   O   E   E
C A P E   C O R R I D O R
K   L   T   F   M       H
T E E T E R   R E T I N A
H       R   P   D   L   G
E N L A R G E D   S L A G
W   E   I   L   C   I   A
H A T E F U L   O C C U R
I   U   I   E   O   I   D
P O P O C A T E P E T L
```

188

```
M O N M O U T H S H I R E
A   O   C   H   W   N   R
G U N   C A R P A C C I O
M   P   A   I   N   O   S
A B R A S I V E   A N T I
    O   I   E   R   S   O
R E D H O T   L E G I O N
O   U   N   V   S   D
B A C H   F A R E W E L L
O   T   H   L   A   R   O
T R I C O L O U R   A R C
I   V   L   U   C   T   K
C H E D D A R C H E E S E
```

SOLUTIONS

189

B	A	C	T	E	R	I	A	L		C		P
	W		I		I		P		P	U	M	A
G	R	A	N	D	P	R	I	X		R		C
	Y		T		P		E		H	I	G	H
A		R		S	L	I	C	K		O		Y
S	E	E	T	H	E		E	R	A	S	E	D
S		P		A			I		I		E	
A	D	R	I	F	T		U	L	S	T	E	R
I		I		T	W	I	R	L		Y		M
L	A	M	B		I		B		E		S	
A		A		S	T	R	A	N	G	E	L	Y
N	I	N	E		C		N		G		I	
T		D		T	H	R	E	E	S	O	M	E

190

P	A	R	A	S	O	L		F		P		B
L		O		A		A	L	A	M	O	D	E
O	R	G	A	N	I	C		I		P		A
Y		E		C		T	O	R	R	E	N	T
S	P	R	A	T		I		A		Y		I
	O			I	N	C	O	N	C	E	R	T
	L		M			D			O			
C	O	M	P	O	S	E	R	S		C		
R		I		N		V		Q	U	A	K	E
A	S	C	R	I	B	E		U		R		X
B		R		O		N	E	A	R	E	S	T
B	R	O	G	U	E	S		R		N		O
Y		N		S		O	V	E	R	A	L	L

191

			S	A	R	C	A	S	T	I	C
S		F		T		U		L		H		R
P	L	A	T	E		S	U	P	R	E	M	O
E		M		E		T		S		W		S
A	C	I	D	R	A	I	N		K	I	S	S
K		L		A		C		C		N		C
V	O	Y	A	G	E		H	O	O	D	O	O
O		D		E		M		U		Y		U
L	O	O	T		C	O	R	S	I	C	A	N
U		C		P		N		C		I		T
M	O	T	T	L	E	D		O	T	T	E	R
E		O		A		E		U		Y		Y
S	T	R	E	N	U	O	U	S			

192

E	L	V	I	S	C	O	S	T	E	L	L	O
	I		D		H		W		R		I	
O	N	C	E		A	P	I	A	R	I	E	S
	O		A		R		N		A		S	
F	L	A	S	H	L	I	G	H	T			
E			I		I			I			A	
H	U	M	B	L	E		A	L	C	O	V	E
	M		A			B					E	
		C	H	L	O	R	O	F	O	R	M	
	C		K		A		I		I		S	
M	A	R	O	O	N	E	D		L	O	I	N
	S		U		C		G		T		O	
W	H	I	T	E	E	L	E	P	H	A	N	T

193

V	I	C	E		M	A	C	H	I	S	M	O
I		O			U		O		O		U	
R	O	U	X		D	R	A	U	G	H	T	S
T		N		J		O		S		O		T
U	P	T	H	E	C	R	E	E	K			
O		E		R		A		B		J		B
U	P	S	H	O	T		C	O	L	O	U	R
S		S		M		D		U		D		I
		H	E	L	I	A	N	T	H	U	S	
T		B		K		V		D		P		T
E	A	U	D	E	V	I	E		H	U	L	L
A		S		R		N			R		E	
M	U	T	I	N	E	E	R		I	S	I	S

194

	F	R	A	T	R	I	C	I	D	E	
O		D		O		U		E		B	
P	R	I	M	E	V	A	L		F	I	R	M
U		I		E		L		E		E	
M	A	R	X		J	O	U	R	N	A	L
	E		A		D			S		
E	N	D	O	R	S	E	M	E	N	T
X			T		N		A		
S	P	U	T	N	I	K		U	R	G	E
E		O		S		P		H		X	
B	R	O	W		T	E	A	P	A	R	T	Y
T		E		E		T		R		R	
	B	R	U	S	C	H	E	T	T	A	

195

	M	A	S	C	A	R	P	O	N	E
A		O		R		E		U		
C	L	O	B	B	E	R		T	O	P	I	C
C		S		I		E		T		O	
E	Y	E	D		O	V	E	R	K	I	L	L
N			I		E		P		A		E	
T	H	R	A	S	H		W	A	L	L	O	P
U		E		O		K		N			O	
A	P	P	A	L	L	E	D		S	L	U	R
T		L		A		A		M		I		T
E	L	I	O	T		T	R	O	U	N	C	E
		C		E		O		A		E	
	P	A	D	D	I	N	G	T	O	N

196

S	C	O	R	C	H	E	R		C	H	A	P
O		U		O		N		B		E		R
O	F	T	E	N		O	R	E	G	A	N	O
N		C		F		U		Y		R		T
	B	A	K	I	N	G	P	O	W	D	E	R
F		S		R		H		N			U	
A	U	T	U	M	N		E	D	I	T	E	D
N			A		S		B		O		E	
C	O	N	S	T	I	T	U	E	N	C	Y	
I		Y		I		R		L		C		F
F	U	L	S	O	M	E		I	D	A	H	O
U		O		N		W		E		T		N
L	Y	N	X		U	N	A	F	R	A	I	D

SOLUTIONS

197

(grid 197)

P	O	M	P		A	S	S	E	S	S	E	D
R		A		W		L		X		E		E
O	F	F	L	I	N	E		P	I	Q	U	E
V		I		T		I		E		U		R
E	X	A	C	T		G	A	L	L	O	N	
R			E		H			I		S		
B	E	F	O	R	E	T	H	E	M	A	S	T
S		L		O		X				U		
	M	A	S	S	I	F		P	O	K	E	R
G		T		T		H		O		E		G
O	S	T	I	A		A	B	S	E	N	C	E
L		E		R		N		E		Y		O
F	I	R	E	S	I	D	E		V	A	I	N

198

(grid 198)

J	A	R	R	O	W		B	A	R	R	O	W
I		A		P		R		A		A		
G	L	I	N	T		R	E	B	U	K	E	D
S		S		I		I		O		E		I
A	L	I	G	N	E	D		R	I	S	E	N
W		N				I						G
	G	E	T	A	C	R	O	S	S			
S			A		U			N		A		
T	H	R	O	B		L	A	M	P	O	O	N
R		I		A		E		A		O		D
A	D	V	I	S	E	D		M	A	K	E	R
I		E		C			B		E		E	
N	A	R	R	O	W		M	A	R	R	O	W

199

(grid 199)

		F		S		G		S			
	C	O	L	D	H	E	A	R	T	E	D
	O		E		O		M		A		O
A	G	E	D		R	U	M	I	N	A	N	T
N			T		A		D		E	
B	O	S	W	E	L	L		F	O	R	T	Y
S		I		Y		N		U		O	
S	C	E	N	E		B	E	S	T	M	A	N
E		D		T		U				T	
S	N	A	P	S	H	O	T		S	O	U	P
T		I		I		R		L		R	
	I	M	P	R	E	C	A	T	I	O	N
		E		F		L		P			

200

(grid 200)

		W		S		W		C			
	F	O	R	T	N	I	G	H	T		
A		O		O		N		U		I	
A	B	E	D		L	I	N	I	M	E	N	T
Y		W		I		E				S	
E	S	P	I	E	D		R	A	R	I	T	Y
S		N				E		A			
M	I	N	D	E	D		F	U	M	I	N	G
N		E		E		E		E		T	
H	I	G	H	B	A	L	L		M	I	L	K
A		A		R		L			B		Y
	A	U	C	T	I	O	N	E	D		
		L		H		W		R			

201

```
W I N K L E P I C K E R S
O O E   Y   U   A   P
W A R R A N T   L E G A L
  F K   H   D   L   E
C O O L ■ F O R E S E E N
O   L   S   N   S   D
M A K E U P   G A U C H O
P   P   B   C   O   U
L E S S E N E D ■ O M A R
I   C   R   L   Z   M
C O R G I ■ I N E X A C T
I   E   O   E   R   N A
T O W E R O F L O N D O N
```

202

```
  T R I L B Y   C I R C A
  O   N   U   L   E   L
M O R S E L   S E E S A W
  M   U   L   A   I   A
C U R L   E V E R Y D A Y
  C   T   T   M   U   S
  H O S T I L I T I E S ■
S   V   N   L   N   O
C R E V A S S E   C U R T
R   R   R   Z   L   C
O Y S T E R   O L I V E R
L   E   A   L   N   R
L E E D S   S A F E T Y
```

203

```
■ C R O S S S T I T C H ■
P   O E   C   N   E   N
I N T H E M A I N   S E E
E     M   R   E   S   S
C O M B I   C E R E A L S
E   E N   E     T   U
O R A N G E   R A T I O N
F   T     I   R   O   D
C H E V R O N   C A N T O
A   A   O   V   A     R
K I T   S T A N D F I R M
E   E   E   I   I L   A
■ P R E S E N T A B L E ■
```

204

```
B E L U G A ■ B E D B U G
I   H   O   N   L   O H
G R A N D M A   F L U K E
T   S   L   I   I   D T
O V A T E   L I N E O U T
P     S   V   I     O
■ B O G S T A N D A R D ■
S   D     R   A     S
K I D S K I N   S T R U T
E   B   N   I   H   A I
T I A R A   S P O R R A N
C   L   V   H   F   E G
H E L P E R ■ A F F R A Y
```

SOLUTIONS

205

206

207

208

209

```
 DOUBLEBLUFF
EW U X O A O
CONFLICTS IMP
C L E E R E
LOTTO EARLYON
E O C D T A
STOCKY DETAIN
C T U N L D
ATHEIST GUESS
K A C O R H
ETC IMPROMPTU
S H L I S E T
 NEWYEARSDAY
```

210

```
DRAWONESSWORD
 E A U U R E
BLAG RISSOLES
 A E S H N F
STARVELING
 I R U H
AVIARY SUNSET
 E I T L
  MORTADELLA
 B L A R X H
ARRESTED COOK
 I S E O O L
BEDSIDEMANNER
```

211

```
BLAH SHEEPISH
U C A Y B U
ZITS SWEEPING
Z O P A C S S
WAFFLEIRON
O G A I N I N
ROOKIE STANZA
D D N A A D M
  ICEMACHINE
E S H U T R D
PINNACLE TEAR
I U N E C O
COGITATE STEP
```

212

```
 PEJORATIVE
R E O A I C
BOUZOUKI THOU
W E E L A U
LOBE TBILISI
 E S A I
MALFUNCTION
U B K M
BELGIUM SPAT
 S A R O L A
SLOT BESMIRCH
 I O I L E K
 BREAKOFDAY
```

SOLUTIONS

213

214

215

216

217

```
C U T E S T . A B A C U S
H . R . H . . . E . R . P
I B I Z A . P R E Q U E L
R . M . K . U . F . D . A
P O M P O U S . T E E N S
Y . E . . . S . E . . . H
. R U S T Y N A I L . . .
F . . E . F . . . I . . W
R O W A N . O B S C E N E
I . R . E . O . O . D . E
D R A U G H T . F R O C K
G . T . A . . . T . W . L
E X H A L E . S Y D N E Y
```

218

```
. . I . I . S . D
C A B I N E T W O R K
H . E . S . O . G . I
M A R X . T H U G G I S H
N . . E . T . E . S
S N O W M A N . G R I M E
E . H . D . R . E . E
P L A I T . H E A L T H Y
S . T . W . Y . . A
S U Z E R A I N . P U R L
R . L . L . A . A . D
F R I T T E R A W A Y
. E . Z . D . N
```

219

```
. F . L . W . M
. P A R O C H I A L
A . C . O . I . S . U
K N O T . F E T C H I N G
Y . O . A . E . . . S
I S T I T C H . N O R W A Y
A . U . . . O . V
I S K I M P Y . B E C K O N
E . . E . O . K . U
C R U D E O I L . S A R I
S . R . M . E . T . Y
. L U N A R Y E A R
. B . N . N . R
```

220

```
M E A T A N D T W O V E G
A . E . W . O . E . I . U
C U R T A I N . D E L T A
. O . Y . K . G . E . R
C O S H . N E W W O R L D
O . O . H . Y . O . . S
F I L L E T . P O M P O M
F . . A . S . D . O . A
E X C A V A T E . O M E N
E . A . E . E . G . P
C O V E N . R I O T E R S
U . E . L . E . B . I . O
P A R T Y P O L I T I C S
```

SOLUTIONS

221

222

223

224